Ahrends, Burton and Koralek

Twentieth Century Architects

Ahrends, Burton and Koralek

Twentieth Century Architects

Kenneth Powell

© Kenneth Powell, 2012

Published by RIBA Publishing, 15 Bonhill Street,
London EC2P 2EA

ISBN 978 1 85946 1 662

Stock Code 75271

The right of Kenneth Powell to be identified as the Author
of this work has been asserted in accordance with the
Copyright, Designs and Patents Act 1988 Sections 77 and 78.

British Library Cataloguing-in-Publication Data
A catalogue record for this book is available from the British
Library.

Commissioning Editors: Lucy Harbor and Matthew
Thompson
Series Editors: Barnabas Calder, Elain Harwood and Alan
Powers
Production: Neil O'Regan
Copy Editor: Ian McDonald
Typeset by Carnegie Book Production
Printed and bound by W.G. Baird, Antrim

RIBA Publishing is part of RIBA Enterprises Ltd.

www.ribaenterprises.com

Front cover photo: ABK's residential building at Keble
College, Oxford, with William Butterfield's hall in the
background. James O. Davies English Heritage

Back cover photo: Paul Koralek, Peter Ahrends and Richard
Burton walking along the pedestrian bridge at Poplar station
on the Docklands Light Railway. (Photo by Valerie Bennett /
National Portrait Gallery)

Frontispiece: Nebenzahl House, Jerusalem, 1968–72
(photograph by Paul Koralek/AA Photo Library).

Foreword

Peter Ahrends, Richard Burton and Paul Koralek founded their practice, ABK, in 1961, while still in their final year at the Architectural Association (AA). It was their powerful design for a social housing scheme – a beautifully proportioned humanistic interpretation of Le Corbusier's Unité d'Habitation in Marseille – that grabbed my attention then, and has retained it for 50 years.

I remember thinking that if this was the quality of work being produced by students at the AA – the only school in Britain teaching modern architecture rather than classicism at that time – then British architecture had an exciting and thriving future ahead of it. How wrong I was!

ABK's roots are in the birth of a new, socially-engaged and optimistic architecture in the years after the Second World War. In those grey days, architects worked with politicians and social scientists to try to create a better society in our damaged cities.

The Festival of Britain in 1951, held on London's South Bank, was a watershed for British Modernism, but it was just the most prominent expression of a maelstrom of creativity, much of which was to be found in local authority architects' offices (now sadly things of the past). ABK was born out of this maelstrom.

From the outset, ABK developed a clear architectural language, but also a socially-engaged style that reflected their origins. Their beautiful studio, in a mews off Primrose Hill, was a meeting place for many friends and collaborators, a place where ideas could be exchanged and talks given in a calm atmosphere. At Richard Rogers Partnership (RRP), we sought to create the same ethos of social responsibility and engagement.

ABK's approach is genuinely collaborative. Their buildings are designed as a team, and cannot be attributed to one or other of the partners. The Berkeley Library at Trinity College, Dublin, was the competition-winning scheme that brought the partners together in 1961, and remains an outstanding building. It is calm, quiet and beautifully proportioned, a jewel sitting comfortably in well-designed public space, and a building with a genuinely human scale. The Berkeley Library is a milestone in British and Irish architecture.

Amongst their most successful English works are the De Breyne and Hayward buildings for Keble College, Oxford, which include student accommodation and a semi-sunken student bar. Designed by ABK in the early seventies, the buildings underline the practice's subtle understanding of how to marry old and new, and their ability to work on awkward sites. One of my sons studied at Keble and I came to know and love the ABK buildings, with their sinuous curves (which later became a hallmark of ABK's architecture) and the string of vertical rhythms of the brick towers.

opposite: John Lewis, Kingston upon Thames

RRP's and ABK's paths crossed a number of times. The most memorable and momentous was in 1984 when we were both shortlisted for the extension of the National Gallery on Trafalgar Square. ABK won the competition with a beautiful design, using a scale and palette of materials that responded to the existing National Gallery, without resorting to imitation. The design was elegantly modern, with a small piazza that brilliantly separated their building from William Wilkins' 1832 gallery.

In May of the same year, Prince Charles made an unprecedented attack on modernist architecture at the 150th anniversary of the Royal Institute of British Architects (RIBA) Royal Gala Evening at Hampton Court Palace. With scant reference to Charles Correa, who won the RIBA Gold Medal that year, the Prince launched his assault on modern architecture, describing the ABK design as a 'monstrous carbuncle on the face of a much-loved and elegant friend.' The scheme was never taken forward and a few years later, the American architect Robert Venturi won a closed competition with a pastiche of the existing gallery.

The Prince's intervention seriously damaged the standing of ABK, an exceptionally talented and sensitive practice, so much so that their work flow was dramatically affected. RRP felt the impact too: some of the media decided that the Prince was referring to our scheme rather than ABK's winning scheme, but we felt we were in good company as the victims of the Prince's unaccountable and ill-informed judgements. (As a footnote, some years later the BBC, RIBA and Royal Academy tried to set up a debate on modernism with the Prince and I was asked to participate. From Buckingham Palace the reply came, 'the Prince does not debate'.)

Paul Koralek has written that 'architecture is about people and their lives, about making spaces that will have a living dynamic, a significant relationship with the life and activity that they will contain'. The buildings that he and his partners have created over the past decades are true and lasting expressions of this humanistic belief.

Richard Rogers

Acknowledgements

Peter Ahrends, Richard Burton and Paul Koralek have given freely of their time over many months to discuss, expound and reminisce about the extraordinary variety of projects which passed through their office in half a century of practice. They have been constantly at hand to answer my questions, and I hope they feel their efforts have been appropriately rewarded in this book. My researches were assisted, as ever, by the staff of the RIBA Library and Drawings Collection and I would like to thank Robert Elwall and Jonathan Makepeace in particular for their help. Valerie Bennett at the Architectural Association provided access to the large collection of ABK images housed in the AA photo library. Sue Harding provided invaluable assistance with the preparation of the project list. James O. Davies of English Heritage visited a number of the buildings more than once to provide a stunning collection of new images. I am grateful to Elain Harwood and Alan Powers for their encouragement and advice, and to Robert Davys for advice on recent Irish projects. Finally, the book reflects the expert guidance and painstaking work of Sharon Hodgson, Neil O'Regan and Matthew Thompson at RIBA Publishing. The practice would like to commend the collaboration between RIBA, English Heritage and the Twentieth Century Society.

This book has been made possible by donations from the following:

John Lewis Partnership

Norman and Underwood (Jon Castleman)

Miller Roofing (Alan Hilditch)

Reflex–Rol UK (Dick de Leeuw)

The Collen family

TWENTIETH CENTURY SOCIETY

C20

Without the Twentieth Century Society an entire chapter of Britain's recent history was to have been lost. It was alert when others slept. It is still crucial!

Simon Jenkins, writer, historian, journalist

The Twentieth Century Society campaigns for the preservation of architecture and design in Britain from 1914 onwards and is a membership organisation which you are warmly invited to join and support.

The architecture of the twentieth century has shaped our world and must be part of our future; it includes bold, controversial, and often experimental buildings that range from the playful Deco of seaside villas to the Brutalist concrete of London's Hayward Gallery. The Twentieth Century Society joined this collaborative series of monographs as part of its campaigning work. We seek to research the work of key architects of our period, to offer an enjoyable and accessible guide for novice and enthusiast, and to use the books to help make the case for why these buildings should be conserved.

Previous volumes in the series have already had a major impact. Our nomination of "British Brutalism" to the 2012 World Monuments Watch was successful in part due to Alan Clawley's *John Madin* focusing on Birmingham's Central Library as this architect's outstanding work. The recent Oxford Dictionary of National Biography has also followed our lead and included entries on Donald McMorran (of *McMorran & Whitby*) and Gordon Ryder (of *Ryder & Yates*).

We propose buildings for listing, advise on restoration and help to find new uses for buildings threatened with demolition. Join the Twentieth Century Society and not only will you help to protect these modern treasures, you will also gain an unrivalled insight into the groundbreaking architecture and design that helped to shape the century though our magazine journal and events programme.

For further details and on line membership details see *www.c20society.org.uk.*

CATHERINE CROFT

DIRECTOR

opposite: Redcar Library, completed in 1971, demolished in 2011

Introduction

The practice of Ahrends, Burton & Koralek occupies a unique position in the history of architecture in post-war Britain. The partnership of Peter Ahrends, Richard Burton and Paul Koralek, all three born in 1933, was established in 1961. The early 1960s was an optimistic era. Britain remained a major industrial nation, though still bearing in places the scars of the Second World War, and a more equal one than it had been in the pre-war years. In 1964 Harold Wilson's Labour Government came to power – a cause for celebration in the ABK office.

The founders of the practice were schooled in the tradition of architecture as social service. After five years at the Architectural Association (AA), two of them, Richard Burton and Paul Koralek, worked for Powell & Moya, at the time probably the most respected of British architectural practices and one with a proud record of building housing, schools and hospitals. Powell & Moya was a creation of the immediate post-war period, but in 1961 figures such as Leslie Martin, Basil Spence, Denys Lasdun (for whom Peter Ahrends worked for a time) and Ernö Goldfinger, who had all practised in the heroic pre-war years when the Modern Movement rooted itself in Britain, were still actively at work. During the 1960s the public sector remained a major source of work for architects, including the youthful office of ABK, with the housing and school-building programmes of the 1950s continuing and with exciting openings provided by the development of the new universities and the expansion of the higher-education sector in general – the degree to which Oxford and Cambridge, for example, were transformed in this period, both architecturally and socially, is frequently overlooked. Alongside continued investment in the public sector, the commercial scene was buoyant, though the architects of the new shopping centres and office blocks trans-forming the look of British cities were a distinct breed, somewhat despised by the architectural elite and cold-shouldered by the critics.

A new generation of architects, including James Stirling and James Gowan, Alison and Peter Smithson, Colin St John Wilson, and the partners in Howell Killick Partridge and Amis, all born in the 1920s, their early careers stunted by the war and its aftermath, had begun to make their mark in the late 1950s – Stirling and Gowan's Leicester engineering block, designed in the late 1950s and completed in 1963, was something of an inspiration for ABK. For Peter Ahrends, 'the Leicester building caused more than a slight pause over a mug of coffee and cigarettes. That "object", in bringing together all of its distinctive parts, offered a magically beautiful new assembly ... it was the shock of the new, of a beautifully made set of ideas that mattered so much at Leicester.'[1] The

opposite: **The British Embassy occupies a prominent position on the banks of the Moscow River**

impact of Leicester can clearly be seen in Ahrends' addition to Keble College, Oxford. Stirling and Gowan's work was a clear source for the fledgling school of High Tech, emerging in the architecture of Team 4, formed by Norman Foster and Richard Rogers in 1962, and in that of the partnership of Terry Farrell and Nicholas Grimshaw. Under the leadership of Foster and Rogers, High Tech was to dominate the British architectural scene for three decades. ABK, however, retained its own trajectory, its work being 'difficult to categorise, for it boasts neither the consistency associated with a single dominant designer, nor that resulting from the dogged pursuit of a constant theoretical viewpoint'.[2] Foster and Rogers, like the founders of ABK, were influenced in their youth by the work of Frank Lloyd Wright, but Wright remained an influence on the work of ABK to a degree that was not apparent in the later work of Foster and Rogers and their followers. Wright's influence, Peter Blundell Jones has written, was at the root of 'ABK's interest in space and light as opposed to form, in process as much as product, in architecture as the unpredicted outcome of specific conditions, rather than as the imposition of a preconceived notion'.[3]

Fundamental to ABK's work over nearly five decades was the idea of partnership and collaboration. The three founding partners were all active designers and the projects they ran bear their individual stamps. (This is not to diminish the role of the other partners and associates in the practice – the late Paul Drake, for example, who joined ABK soon after its foundation, was also a highly able designer.) At the same time, every project, from the Berkeley Library onwards, has benefited from the input of all three partners. Working as a group was also a basic ingredient of ABK's approach from the beginning – in 1971 Richard Burton explained that 'over the years we have developed what might be termed "group territory": that is, a common pool of word associations, experience, ideas and behaviour. We are agile in such territory.'[4] John Donat, who photographed much of ABK's work and was a close friend of the partners, wrote that 'an ABK building is recognizable not through any family resemblance of style, appearance or manner, but because what they build comes through a process of decision and selection specific to each job, but characterized by their own particular way of solving (and sometimes creating) problems'.[5] Donat stressed the 'personal and particular' nature of ABK's architecture, its promotion of individuality over universally applied solutions. This characteristic feature of the firm's work is apparent in those projects where there is an obvious response to context: the series of additions to Trinity College, Dublin; Keble College; the Oxford chaplaincy; and the unbuilt National Gallery extension, for example.

There are other key characteristics which emerge across the spectrum of ABK's work. The pursuit of social benefit is a basic tenet which has driven the practice since its foundation. Even as ABK was getting into its stride in the 1960s, some of the preconceptions which had driven the Modern Movement from its beginning were being questioned – architects were not yet the villains that the conservative critics of the 1980s sought to paint them as, but their visions were increasingly suspect. Interest began to focus on the impact of buildings on the lives of their users, particularly in the field of housing. Architects and planners were no longer assumed to know best. ABK was to take a lead in the new agenda of consultation – tenants of its housing at Basildon helped to shape the next phases of development in the town. The employees of Cummins were able to build into the new factory at Shotts features which enhanced their own working lives. Inspirational clients such as Lyall Collen, J. Irwin Miller, John Hester, Derry Shanley and Norman Leyland played a key role in shaping projects. The physical form of ABK's buildings reflects the social aspirations of the architecture. The great glazed roofs of the Portsmouth and Redcar libraries, the John Lewis store at Kingston and the unrealised British Telecom headquarters continue the theme of using natural light which was present in the Berkeley Library and the library at the Chichester Theological College but are also an element in the creation of democratic social spaces which contrast with the hierarchy imposed by compartmentalisation.

In many respects, ABK's work can be seen as part of a renewal of Modernism in the face of increasingly vocal criticism of its past achievements stemming from environmentalists, advocates of community involvement and conservationists. When ABK was commissioned to design a heritage centre in Dover it responded with a building (the White Cliffs Experience) which incorporated a retained Victorian façade and managed to be 'well mannered and fastidiously dressed … distinctly Classical, though in an utterly contemporary manner'.[6] (A failure as an 'experience', the building was later adapted to house the local public library and museum.) ABK's premiated design for the extension to London's National Gallery managed to achieve the same balance of traditional decorum and modernity – the meddling of some of the Gallery's trustees drained the project of some of its most distinctive features and led to its eventual demise.

Involvement with the visual arts was always important to ABK, from the days of its early projects for the Marlborough and Kasmin galleries. It was a cause that Richard Burton in particular, with his close family ties to the art world, always championed. Burton was able to make the incorporation of works of art a major feature of St Mary's Hospital and the British Embassy in Moscow. He was equally active in progressing the practice's ongoing environmental concerns, endorsing the call of RIBA President Alex Gordon for architecture embodying the principles of 'long life/low energy/loose fit'. The energy crisis of the early 1970s made architects aware of the imperative to design in tune with the natural environment, and ABK's response was apparent in the W. H. Smith and Cummins projects and the later phases of their housing at Basildon. In 2008, Burton delivered a lecture at the RIBA in which he expounded a holistic view of architecture as part of 'our physical and psychological survival kit'. Schools of architecture, he argued, 'should major on all these issues relating to survival and sustainability with specific acknowledgment of the importance of understanding nature and natural forces'.[7]

Badly wounded by the abandonment of the National Gallery project, ABK's very survival might have seemed for a time in doubt. The practice was very much rooted in Britain, but had effectively launched itself in Ireland, a country where the pronouncements of the Prince of Wales carried little weight. Ireland proved a lifeline, generating a series of excellent civic and educational buildings, designed increasingly from ABK's

Dublin office, in the wake of the development boom of the 1990s and early 2000s. These projects have a distinctive character of their own yet they all embody qualities which have been present in ABK's buildings from the inception of the practice. The fiftieth anniversary of the partnership is an appropriate time to reassess its contribution to British architecture over the last half century.

Notes

1   Peter Ahrends, in Alan Berman (ed.), *Jim Stirling and the Red Trilogy: three radical buildings*, London, Frances Lincoln, 2010, pp.97–8.

2   Peter Blundell Jones, introduction to *Ahrends Burton and Koralek*, London, Academy Editions, 1991, p.7.

3   ibid., p.8.

4   'Small group design and the idea of quality', *RIBA Journal*, June 1971, p.232.

5   *Architecture Plus*, September/October 1974, p.101.

6   Martin Spring, 'Fresh Dover soul', *Building*, 26 April 1991, p.53.

7. Richard Burton, 'Putting Humpty together', lecture delivered at the RIBA, 24 February 2008.

top: John Wheatley College, Glasgow, 2005–7
opposite: The prototype house at Hooke Park, designed with Frei Otto

1   Origins and Influences

The practice of Ahrends Burton & Koralek was formally established in London by Peter Ahrends, Richard Burton and Paul Koralek in 1961. In reality, however, the partnership was formed some years earlier, when Ahrends, Burton and Koralek began working together as students at the Architectural Association School, where all three enrolled in 1951. It was Paul Koralek's success in the competition for a new library for Trinity College, Dublin – a project subsequently developed with the close involvement of both Ahrends and Burton – that allowed ABK to open an office and recruit staff.

All three partners were born in 1933. Peter Ahrends was a native of Berlin, where both his father and grandfather, Bruno, were architects. Ahrends' father and mother (a weaver) were firmly committed to the ideals of the Bauhaus and to some extent to the vision of a socialist future. Although not committed communists, they had for a time worked in the Soviet Union as part of a team of German designers assembled by Walter Gropius's disciple, Ernst May. The rise of Hitler, which saw the architectural practice established by Bruno Ahrends forcibly closed down, drove Ahrends' father, Steffen – a non-religious Jew, married to a Gentile – to look for a way out of Germany. Fortunately, Steffen Ahrends' brother was already established in South Africa. Steffen joined him, and in 1937 the whole family was able to settle there. Peter Ahrends was in due course sent to a boarding school in East London, having been baptised as a Roman Catholic. He disliked the place and one Sunday ran away to Johannesburg, jumping on a train without a ticket. He was caught and taken to a police station, where he received a severe ticking off before being sent back to school (from which he was summarily expelled). He recalls vividly the rather more severe treatment meted out to another fare-dodger – a young black man – who was beaten by the police. Even in the days before apartheid legalised racial discrimination, Ahrends was aware of the injustices of South African society and the fact that there seemed to be one law for white people, another for blacks. Lacking formal qualifications, having finished school at a young age, the 16-year-old proved to be an able craftsman – 'I got the sense of what it was like to be a worker', he recalls. He trained as a carpenter and plumber, and helped his father with the construction of a new house.

Ahrends had already decided to leave South Africa, and a colleague of his father suggested the AA as the best place to study architecture. His passage to England was leisurely, firstly via an Italian ship which deposited him in Venice, where he spent a week – an extraordinary reintroduction to Europe. After a few weeks staying with family friends in Florence, Ahrends travelled by train to London, where he lived for

opposite: Peter Ahrends, Richard Burton and Paul Koralek at Richard Burton's wedding in 1956

N W   E L E V A T I O N

a time with another friend of the family, a doctor, before moving into a bedsit in a distinctly unglamorous Notting Hill. The Festival of Britain was in full swing and Ahrends was excited by its 'sense of optimism and purpose'. The AA was equally exciting, with inspiring teachers and a strong commitment to the idea of architecture as an engine of social change which was in tune with the young South African's thinking. In the first year at the AA, Ahrends got to know Burton and Koralek.

Richard Burton had a close family connection with the Festival of Britain: his stepfather, Gerald Barry (1898–1968), was Director General of the Festival. Formerly editor of the *News Chronicle*, and probably the youngest editor on Fleet Street in his time, Barry was a passionate supporter of the Modern Movement and had employed F. R. S. Yorke to design extensions to his country retreat, Forge House, in Sussex, before the Second World War. (Burton's early years had been spent in Yorke's first house, 'Torilla', at Hatfield, commissioned by his paternal grandmother, Christabel Burton.) At Forge House, Burton met Hugh Casson and other architects working on the Festival and it was here, he recalls, that Gerald Barry suggested he study architecture. Burton's mother, Vera, who married Barry, the second of her three husbands, in 1944, was born in St Petersburg, the daughter of a Russian émigré, Vladimir Poliakoff, a civil engineer who had quit Russia in 1917. In London, Poliakoff, nicknamed 'Polly' (who had got to know Lenin through his position as an interpreter for the British mission), had established himself as a successful journalist and, in the 1930s, became a well-informed and vociferous critic of the policy of appeasement. Burton was close to his grandfather, who encouraged him to study architecture. Burton's father, Basil, was Anglo-Irish and his grandmother was a Harmsworth, a scion of the famous newspaper dynasty. Basil Burton owned the Academy Cinema on Oxford Street, for long London's most notable 'art house' cinema – 'I was raised on films', says Burton.

Burton 'learned a certain amount' about architecture while a schoolboy at Bryanston. A talk given at the school by Philip Powell, later to employ Burton at Powell & Moya, 'set my enthusiasm alight', as he later recalled. At Bryanston, encouraged by some excellent teachers, Burton continued to develop his skills as a painter – he spent holidays in the South of France and in St Ives, where Ben Nicholson was his mentor.

above: Peter Ahrends' student project drawing for housing at Gallchoille on the west coast of Scotland

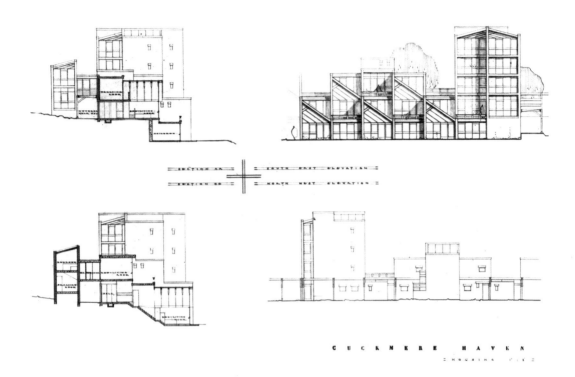

CUCKMERE HAVEN

above: **Richard Burton's student project for a school at Cuckmere, Sussex**

He has never stopped painting, and even when in his first year at the AA took drawing classes at the Slade School with William Coldstream. But painting would never be more than a leisure pursuit: 'I wanted to be an architect from the start', Burton recalls, 'and never wavered in that ambition.' After working for a time in the Festival of Britain offices, he was able to enter the AA shortly before his eighteenth birthday in 1951.

Paul Koralek was born in Vienna. He came to London in 1938 when his Jewish parents quit Austria – his father was interned for a time on the Isle of Man as an enemy alien. At the age of five he was sent to a progressive school run by a German émigré, where enlightened teachers instilled in him an interest in the visual arts. At the age of eleven, following a spell as an evacuee in rural Herefordshire, he went on to Aldenham School in Hertfordshire. The main thrust of the school at that time was training boys to enter the civil service, but Koralek received a good general education. He loved drawing and conceived the idea of training as an architect – 'I always seemed to be drawing houses', he says. A neighbour of his parents recommended the AA, but Koralek was barely seventeen and too young to enrol in the school. Anticipating a custom which was to become almost universal in later decades, he took a 'year off', spending a year in Paris with a French family. He was able to register for courses at the Sorbonne, studying French culture, art history, painting and sculpture, and becoming fluent in the French language. It was clearly a magical time, but at the end of the year Koralek returned to London and to the AA.

The AA in 1951 was a place of high ideals, though the arrival of Ahrends, Burton and Koralek virtually coincided with the departure of Robert Furneaux Jordan, the popular (and passionately left-wing) head of the school – the students called an emergency meeting to protest about his removal and the appointment of Michael Patrick in his place. There were still students who had returned to the school after war service – they seemed very mature to the younger generation. The Festival was inspirational, but relatively little was being built in Britain. Ahrends, Burton and Koralek had Leonard Manasseh as their first year master – he was, recalls Peter Ahrends, 'very endearing but also very businesslike'. The first project set by Manasseh and his assistant Olive Sullivan was the design of a classic 'primitive hut'. During the next five years, the three young men were exposed to some outstanding teachers – Felix Samuely for structures, for example, and John Summerson lecturing on architectural history – who were to influence their formation as architects. One of the most memorable was Arthur Korn (1891–1978), who had come to London from Germany in 1938 as a refugee from Nazism. He began teaching at the AA in 1945 and remained a tutor there for the next 20 years. He was forthright in his comments on student projects – 'I hate ziss thing!'

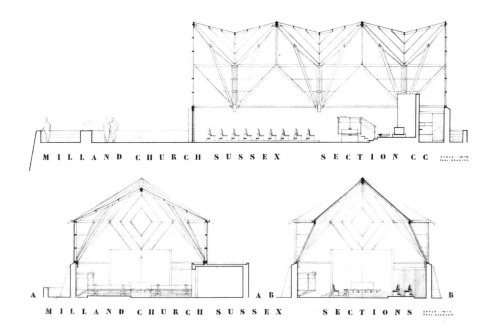

above: Paul Koralek's student project for a church at Milland, Hants

he exclaimed as one model was unveiled – but he could be generous with praise too. 'He was quite capable of saying "I love ziss thing"', says Ahrends. Korn had known Peter Ahrends' grandfather, Bruno – both had been associated with 'Der Ring', the group founded in Berlin by Gropius in 1925 to campaign for the new architecture of Modernism. All three partners in the future ABK remember Korn as a great and charismatic teacher. 'He was hugely emotional', says Koralek, 'and believed that you should express your emotions in your work.' Korn's urbanistic thinking, which emphasised the organic nature of urban development, was to influence ABK.

Although the Festival of Britain had been a 'tonic for the nation', raising the spirits of young architects, the picturesque, 'soft' approach to modern design, Scandinavian in spirit, which it appeared to represent was anathema to a new generation who formed the advance guard of the New Brutalism. As Alan Powers has remarked, the transition from the Festival idiom to the New Brutalism as a dominant influence on British architecture was not the abrupt revolution depicted by some critics favourable to the latter tendency.[1] Powell & Moya, Yorke Rosenberg and Mardall, Gollins Melvin Ward and the Architects' Co-Partnership (ACP) were responsible for work during the 1950s that while in no sense 'Brutalist', did not lack rigour. All the founding partners of ACP, a practice established on the principle of collaboration, taught at the AA in the 1950s – Paul Koralek particularly remembers Kenneth Capon as an excellent teacher in his second year at the school. Also active in the school were three young architects then working at the London County Council (LCC), Bill Howell, John Killick and John Partridge, who were to form a partnership in 1959. At the LCC, they worked as a team on the Alton West housing at Roehampton, taking inspiration from Le Corbusier's Unité d'Habitation in Marseilles, an icon much admired by the New Brutalists. Howell, in particular, was close to the leading lights of the New Brutalism, the husband-and-wife team of Peter and Alison Smithson – Peter Smithson was unit master during Ahrends', Burton's and Koralek's fifth year at the AA. Alison and Peter Smithson's most influential building, the school at Hunstanton, Norfolk, a radical restatement of Miesian values, was completed in late 1953. For the 'Hards', the Swedish taste reflected in the earlier Alton East estate was unpalatably sentimental and retrograde – the true spirit of the Modern Movement, argued the Smithsons, Howell and others, had been lost and needed to be rediscovered. By the later 1950s, it was being revisited, with spectacular effect, by James Stirling and James Gowan, whose engineering block at Leicester University went on site in 1959. Ahrends, Burton and Koralek found themselves somewhat at odds with the Brutalist ethos of the AA in the mid-1950s. In fact, as John Miller has pointed out, 'when this period at the AA was designated "Brutalist", no account was taken of the diversity of interest that existed in the school'.[2]

Part of this diversity was reflected in the work of the future partners of ABK. 'We seemed to be out on a limb', says Koralek, who was enthused by the work of Frank Lloyd Wright and his *lieber Meister* Louis Sullivan, sharing with Ahrends and Burton a taste for the Gothic – a joint AA project was a measured drawing of part of Salisbury Cathedral. Koralek was inspired by Sullivan's humanistic, spiritual view of architecture.

Sullivan may have invented the axiom 'form follows function', but his view of design was anything but mechanistic or utilitarian. As Koralek commented many years later, 'functionalism is not a style. Nor is it a rejection of ornament. It is an attitude to the search for form, the relationship of form to content, or meaning, which is all-embracing and can relate the many different aspects of design.'[3]

The 'country boys', as Ahrends, Burton and Koralek were nicknamed at the AA, had an unfashionable regard for Wright's early Prairie Houses. Wright was certainly a far more potent influence for them than Le Corbusier, though the pilgrimage chapel at Ronchamp was a revelation – they warmed to the irrationality of a building which shocked some of Corbusier's admirers and, with friends from the AA, hired a minibus and drove off to see the chapel soon after its completion. Frank Lloyd Wright was in his seventies when the RIBA belatedly awarded him the Royal Gold Medal in 1941. He had visited London on the eve of the Second World War and handed out prizes at the AA, telling the students that few of them were likely to succeed as architects. He came again in 1950, at the invitation of Furneaux Jordan, who believed that 'there was only one great architect in the world, and he felt that his students ought to see him'.[4] The students lionised him, giving the lie to the idea that Wright was a minimal influence on the post-war generation in Britain. Nonetheless, the 'country boys' were unusual in their passionate commitment to Wrightian ideas. Wright came to Britain again in 1956, a few years before his death, 'looking for ideas', he said, and Ahrends and Burton encountered the great man in person. From their second year at the AA on, Ahrends, Burton and Koralek worked together on projects, and the idea of a partnership was formed. In the process, an individual approach to design was emerging and the influence of Wright, though still present, became less obvious.

The AA years saw the future partners forming associations that would be important in the years to come. One key contact was the brilliant young engineer Frank Newby (1926–2001), who was already in partnership with Felix Samuely – Newby was to head the firm after Samuely's death in 1959 and to be the engineer for all ABK's earlier projects. Ahrends', Burton's and Koralek's circle of friends at the AA included John Donat (1933–2004), a contemporary of Burton at Bryanston who worked for a time as an LCC architect but was to make his name as an architectural photographer and to record most of ABK's buildings, David Armstrong, Michael Wolff (later of Wolff Olins) and Edward Cullinan, who came to the AA from Cambridge in the fourth year. Another contemporary, Colin Faber, also a Wright devotee, quit the school after a year, deciding that it had nothing to teach him – he went to Mexico, where he became Félix Candela's assistant. Burton recalls him as a natural high-flyer – 'by contrast, we were plodders, talkers and very serious', he says.

After completing their studies at the AA in 1956, the three young men had to square up to the reality of making a living. They were lucky enough, however, to have secured a scholarship which allowed them to travel to the Near East, Turkey and Persia for five months to study Islamic architecture. Peter Ahrends, who had married while still a student, was anxious to return to South Africa for a time, partly to repay the debt he felt to his father. He and his wife, Liz, decided that they would travel on from the Mediterranean to South Africa overland. A Land Rover and trailer were secured and the party set off. Richard Burton had also married (in 1956) and his wife, Mireille, joined the expedition, as did John Donat. The expedition was a great success. Driving through Turkey, the group discovered the extraordinary tenth-century Armenian church of Aghtamar on an island in Lake Van – today it is a popular tourist site, but in 1956 the only way to get to it was in a small boat owned by a local man. Donat took some fine photographs of the church, which were later published in a scholarly study by an American academic. In Isfahan a local architect and AA alumnus, Ali Baktiar, acted as their host for a six-week stay.

At the end of the tour, Koralek, Donat and Richard Burton slowly returned to London (Mireille Burton had gone back home early, having contracted jaundice), but Peter and Liz Ahrends got a passage on an oil tanker to Mauritius and thence by ship to Cape Town – this was the time of the Suez crisis, and the Suez Canal was closed. It was 1958 before they returned to London, Peter having worked in the interval in his father's office. Back in London, he got a job with the partnership of Slater & Uren, where he worked on the Sanderson Building in Marylebone. A stint with Denys Lasdun, assisting with the St James's Park apartments and Fitzwilliam College projects, followed, along with teaching at the AA and work for Julian Keable.

In the meantime, Burton had found a post in the prestigious architect's department of the LCC, where he stayed for 18 months, finding his work there 'frustrating – I was

above: **ABK in Iran: l.to r. – Ali Baktiar, Paul K, Peter A, Liz Ahrends, Mireille Burton, Richard B, John Donat.**
Taken in August 1956

full of ideas I wanted to pursue', he says. Following a few months in Paris in the studio of Guillaume Gillet, Burton went to work for Powell & Moya – 'it was there I learned to be a practising architect'. Philip Powell and Hidalgo ('Jacko') Moya were to figure significantly in the history of ABK. Burton continues to revere them both. He worked for the practice on the staff housing at Swindon and High Wycombe hospitals. Paul Koralek, who had joined Powell & Moya in 1957, was already at work on the Swindon housing and on hospital projects at Wexham Park, Slough, and Wythenshawe. He was soon to quit the practice for New York, but Burton continued there until 1961. The new housing for Brasenose College, Oxford, completed that year, was a project on which the latter worked closely with Moya, acting as project architect and contributing to the evolution of the final, built scheme – though he insists that it is essentially the work of Philip Powell and Jacko Moya. The latter, says Burton, 'taught me to question everything, take nothing at face value. He would always go back to basics – asking things like "what is a door?".' Peter Ahrends was never formally employed by Powell & Moya but, in addition to teaching at the AA, he collaborated with Burton on the design of the furniture for Brasenose. Norman Leyland, the college's bursar, who was instrumental in commissioning Powell & Moya, was later to become a significant client of ABK at Templeton College.[5]

By the early 1960s Powell & Moya, formed in 1946 when the partners won the competition for the huge Churchill Gardens housing project, was one of Britain's most respected architectural practices. By twenty-first-century standards, however, it was never a large operation – there were never more than 50 staff – and Philip Powell and Jacko Moya had no compunction in turning down commissions they thought could not be tackled alongside existing projects. It was in this way that ABK got the commission to design the new student housing for the theological college at Chichester (where Powell's father was a cathedral canon and where Powell & Moya had designed the Festival Theatre). ABK was to be established as a formal partnership after Paul Koralek won the competition for a new library at Trinity College, Dublin.

Koralek had left Powell & Moya in 1958. He went back to Paris, working as a draughtsman for a small practice there, but found the mood of the city sadly changed – the Algerian war was in progress. From Paris he went to Toronto, finding work with a British architect based there. Toronto in the 1950s was a depressingly provincial place – Koralek longed to work in New York. The Hungarian-born architect Marcel Breuer had moved to the USA in 1937, following two years working in England with F. R. S. Yorke, and had formed a partnership with Walter Gropius. He established his own office in New York in 1941, and in 1953 won the commission for the new UNESCO headquarters in Paris. Koralek travelled to New York and went to see Breuer, aware that there was no shortage of talented young architects lining up to work for him. He was, however, invited to submit his CV and was asked to come in for an interview. The offer of a job followed. Not the least significant of Koralek's credentials was his fluent command of French. Breuer had in hand a massive French project – the design of an entire new ski resort at Flaine in the Alps. Within two weeks, Koralek had been given an American

work permit and had joined the Breuer office (where a colleague was the young Richard Meier). He warmed to Breuer's approach: 'he was really a Beaux Arts man at heart, not a functionalist at all, but someone with a sculptor's approach to form', Koralek recalls. This was apparent in the church for the Benedictine abbey of St John, Collegeville, Minnesota, which was then under construction. Koralek was set to depart for France to work at Flaine when he won the Trinity College competition. He was soon on his way back to London, to establish ABK with Ahrends and Burton. But first he took a few weeks off to travel, visiting some of the key works of Frank Lloyd Wright, including Falling Water, the Johnson Wax complex and Taliesin West. Louis Kahn's Richards Laboratories at the University of Pennsylvania also figured on Koralek's itinerary, and Kahn's work was certainly to influence that of ABK. It was a brief interval before Koralek and his partners got to work on the Berkeley Library designs and with those for the Chichester college (which Ahrends and Burton already had in hand). For all three men, the years of study and formation had finished and the world of independent practice beckoned.

Notes

1   Alan Powers, *Britain: modern architectures in history*, London, Reaktion Books, 2007, p.98.

2   John Miller in James Gowan (ed.), *Projects: Architectural Association, 1946–71*, London, n.d., c.1971, p.31.

3   Paul Koralek, 'Architecture or appearances' in *Ahrends Burton and Koralek*, London, Academy Editions, 1991, p.30.

4   Andrew Saint, 'Wright and Great Britain' in Anthony Alofsin (ed.), *Frank Lloyd Wright: Europe and beyond*, Berkeley and London, University of California Press, 1999, p.136.

5   Kenneth Powell, *Powell & Moya*, London, RIBA Publishing, 2009, pp.55–60.

above: **The three partners in ABK discussing the National Gallery project, early 1980s**

2   Learning and Libraries

It was the commission for the Berkeley Library at Trinity College, Dublin, which allowed the three partners to launch into the world of independent practice. While Paul Koralek was working in the USA, Peter Ahrends and Richard Burton had already secured work for the future partnership. There was, for example, the Bryan Brown house at Thurlestone in Devon, a holiday home for an Oxford don, along with some more minor domestic projects and the installation for an exhibition of Henry Moore's sculpture at the Marlborough New London Gallery in London's Bond Street – the outsize lettering on the street frontage of the gallery was a bold move in such conservative surroundings. Burton's connections to the art world were enhanced by his mother's third marriage, following a divorce from Gerald Barry, to the influential art critic John Russell. Other gallery projects followed, notably the Kasmin Gallery in Bond Street, where Ahrends and Burton created calm interiors, skilfully daylit, in a backland area approached by a long, slightly myste- rious corridor from the street. It was quickly recognised as the best small gallery space in London. But these were small projects – Dublin was a major triumph. Following Paul Koralek's return to England, a partnership agreement was drawn up. 'It was a partnership of three equals', says Koralek, 'and founded on friendship and mutual respect.' These were the foundations of a harmonious working relationship which endured for nearly half a century.

Paul Koralek recalls working on a number of previous competition schemes – 'but I wasn't happy with most of them and rarely submitted an entry', he says. He had doubts about his submission for the Dublin library competition but sent it in anyway, never having seen the site or even visited Ireland. Trinity College had been founded in 1592 as part of the British monarchy's strategy to impose its rule on Ireland and impose a Protestant culture on the Irish people. It was strongly associated into the twentieth century with the Protestant ascendancy – only in 1970 did the Roman Catholic Church lift its formal ban on Catholics enrolling as students. By the 1960s, however, attitudes were changing and 'TCD' was becoming more fully integrated into the cultural and intellectual life of an independent Ireland. The college occupies an extensive site on the south side of Dublin, with a fine complex of buildings dating from the early eight- eenth century onwards. Perhaps the finest of them is the Great Library, begun in 1712 to designs by Thomas Burgh, with its aptly named Long Room, one of the most impressive library interiors anywhere, housing that tourist magnet, the *Book of Kells*.

The library of Trinity College remains one of six copyright libraries receiving every book published in the British Isles – by the 1960s it was acquiring by right some 35,000

opposite: **The Berkeley Library was a radical intervention into the historic campus of Trinity College**

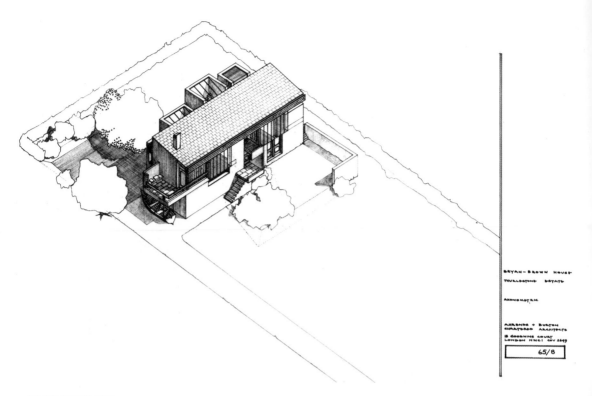

BRYAN-BROWN HOUSE
THURLESTONE ESTATE

AXONOMETRIC

AHRENDS + BURTON
CHARTERED ARCHITECTS
3 GODWINS COURT
LONDON WC1 COV 2449

65/8

top: Perspective of the Bryan Brown House in Devon – ABK's first significant residential project
above left: Super-graphics applied to the Marlborough Gallery for an exhibition of Henry Moore's work
above right: The Kasmin Gallery in London, a project reflecting Richard Burton's links with the art world

books annually. The college was also expanding its student numbers. The pressure on library facilities was growing, and in 1958 Trinity launched an appeal for funds to build a new library – significantly, the Irish Government agreed to match pound for pound the funds raised. With confidence that it could fund the project, the college announced, in 1960, a competition to secure a design for the new building. The new library was to fulfil several roles – providing seats for student and academic readers and also storage for books (space for up to 800,000 volumes was envisaged). The brief was for an extension to the Great Library, overlooking what was then the green enclave of the Fellows' Garden (later to provide a site for ABK's Arts Block) with playing fields to the rear. Koralek, however, saw the possibility of making the new library a separate entity, linked to Burgh's library only at basement level, so preserving the integrity of the historic structure.

The very exacting competition brief (Hugh Casson was one of the assessors) clearly implied that a thoroughly modern building was wanted, one that 'represented the 20th century as well as other college buildings represented the 18th and 19th centuries'. Koralek's winning submission was less Corbusian in mood than the revised scheme as built. 'I won the competition on the basis of the plan', Koralek says. He concedes that the original proposals were 'too spindly – like a collection of sticks'. He had proposed that the building be constructed of precast concrete, but was advised that there was no possibility of an Irish contractor being able to handle a project using that material on a large scale.

top: **President de Valera with Mr Paul Koralek, A.R.I.B.A. (right) winner of the award for the design of the T.C.D. library extension. The Earl of Rosse, Vice-Chancellor, and Dr A. J. McConnell, Provost (left), are in the group**

So the building was redesigned for in-situ concrete construction. The result, says Koralek, was something 'more solid and powerful, in tune with the existing college buildings'. The redesign clearly addressed the concerns of one competition juror, the distinguished Italian architect Franco Albini, that the winning scheme did not 'harmonise with the

above: Interior of the Berkeley Library at Trinity College, Dublin

surroundings or appear to give any indication that the problem of inserting the new architecture within the present surroundings has to be faced'. The built scheme, with Paul Drake as project architect, provided for a powerfully modelled, top-heavy composition which, Alan Colquhoun suggested, had the 'power to suggest a valid sort of monumentality' but 'carries the implication that everything that happens below the top floor is secondary'.[1] Formally opened by the Irish President, Eamon de Valera, on 12 July 1967, the Berkeley Library, as it was named, provided 469 places for readers at a time when Trinity had fewer than 4,000 students. By the 1990s, student numbers had trebled and by 2010 there were more than 16,000 undergraduates and postgraduates.

The brief had demanded a building with scope for expansion, but Koralek was resolutely opposed to the flexible, open-plan diagram represented by Gollins Melvin Ward's university library in Sheffield, opened in 1959 – 'it was exactly what we did not want to do', he says, finding its vast, uniform open-plan spaces inimical to the idea of private study. The Berkeley Library reflects a very different vision – the largest of the reading rooms accommodated just 107 readers. The emphasis was on providing a variety of spaces, each with its own character. The scope for rearranging the interior was limited by, for example, the concrete plinths supporting bookcases and concrete desks and counters. By 1997, the building was judged 'inflexible and a problem for staff

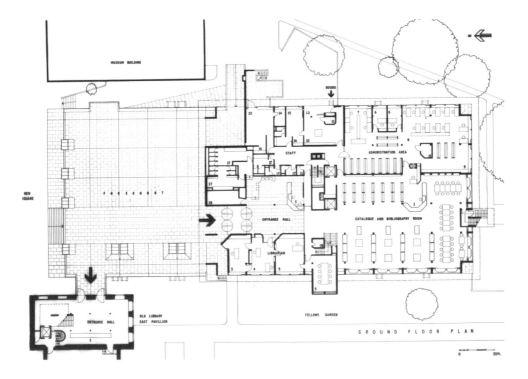

above: **Plan of the Berkeley Library**

with its difficulties made worse by desperate overcrowding'.[2] A subsequent addition removed the pressure on the library, which is widely acclaimed as one of the finest modern buildings in Ireland. The section is the key to the building, with two levels of reading rooms over a ground floor given over to catalogues, reference works and offices. The controlled use of natural light within these working areas is masterly. Equally significant is the creation of a paved forecourt set on a podium which addresses the older buildings of the college and continues the series of squares and courts which characterise its development over the last three centuries. The Berkeley Library still impresses as an extraordinarily mature work for a youthful practice and one, it has been plausibly suggested, which clearly reflects the influence of Louis Kahn as much as that of Corbusier.[3]

Academic and Chaplaincy Work, Chichester and Oxford

The Berkeley Library project was developed from Paul Koralek's competition scheme by the three partners, working in collaboration. From the first, however, the principle was established that, as Koralek remarks, 'we always worked together, but there was always one partner in charge of a project'. In fact, the Chichester Theological College

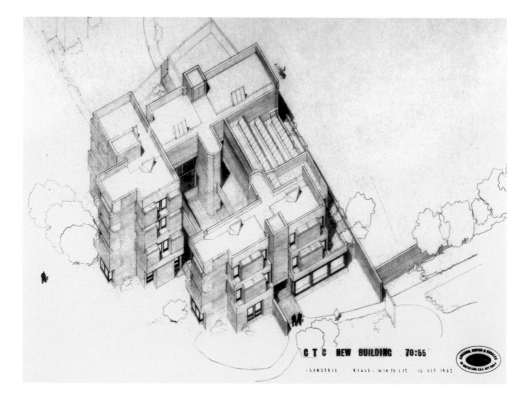

above: Isometric of the Chichester Theological College

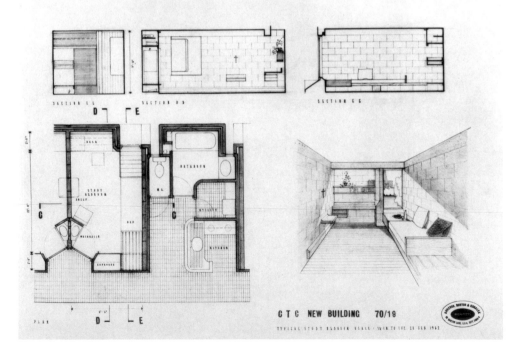

top: Central court of the Chichester Theological College
above: Plan of student rooms

project was being developed by Peter Ahrends and Richard Burton even while Koralek was working on his Dublin competition scheme. Completed in 1965, it provided 35 study bedrooms for students, three small flats for staff, a library and a lecture room, the accommodation arranged around an open court through which passes the route from the older college buildings to the chapel (the former parish church of St Bartholomew). There are memories here of the Brasenose project on which Burton had worked for Powell & Moya, but even more apparent is the influence of Corbusier's Maisons Jaoul, completed in 1956 and something of an icon for the New Brutalist school. Burton concedes the point but stresses that the use of local brick here was a contextual move, a matter of 'fitting in'. The study bedrooms were appropriately austere ('monastic' is Burton's term), with built-in desks and beds making optimum use of a small space and an ingenious use of natural light by means of canted top-lights over the desks. The library at Chichester could be seen as a dry run for the reading rooms in the Berkeley Library – as in so many ABK projects, the manipulation of daylight to create a serene, enjoyable working space is key to its success. Following the closure of the college in 1994, ABK's buildings were converted into sheltered accommodation for the elderly, necessitating some alterations, not all of them sympathetic.

Brick was again used freely for the Roman Catholic Chaplaincy at Oxford, a project led by Peter Ahrends and initially commissioned as early as 1965 but completed only in

above: **Interior of the library**

top: The interior of the Roman Catholic Chaplaincy, side chapel
above: The new chaplaincy building next to the old 'palace' – an example of ABK's concern for historic context

1972 after the brief had been expanded. The chaplaincy was housed in the seventeenth-century Old Palace, off St Aldate's in the heart of the city, but the then (1959–70) university chaplain, Fr Michael Hollings, launched an ambitious plan to greatly improve its facilities and to replace the hut which served as a chapel. Hollings, a dynamic and controversially progressive priest, was fired by the reforms of the Second Vatican Council and wanted a space where Mass could be celebrated, in Vatican II fashion, *coram populo* in the midst of the congregation. The main worship space – there is a smaller chapel for private prayer – is resolutely matter-of-fact, deliberately rejecting any hint of the numinous, its most distinctive feature the circular skylights which fill the interior with diffused daylight. Externally, the stepped façade of the four-storey building, with study bedrooms on the upper floors, provides a strong but sympathetic contrast to that of the Old Palace, and the project provided a positive model for new development in a historic city.

Oxford Centre for Management Studies

Richard Burton's role as project architect for Powell & Moya's additions to Brasenose College, Oxford, was instrumental in securing ABK the commission for the new Oxford Centre for Management Studies. The first director of the Centre was Norman Leyland, the modern-minded bursar of Brasenose who had played a key role in commissioning Powell & Moya. The name was changed to Templeton College in 1984 in recognition of a major benefaction. Leyland approached Powell & Moya to design buildings for the centre on a semi-rural site at Kennington, just outside the city, on land belonging to St John's College, but the practice was simply too busy to take on the job. ABK was recommended as a possible alternative, and the result was a project which was to extend over nearly 30 years in eight phases of work, the first phase completed in 1969 at a cost of just £106,000. The key features of the project, led by Burton throughout with a team that included Peter Wadley, Graham Anthony, Graham Francis and Malcolm McGowan the latter three subsequently partners in the practice of Sheppard Robson, and (for later phases) Malcolm McGowan, were its incremental character, with indefinite expansion provided for, and the client's wish to see a building which reflected its progressive agenda – management studies were a new departure for Oxford University.

In contrast to other Oxford colleges, Templeton provided comprehensive teaching facilities (conference and lecture rooms and library), as well as residential accommodation and social spaces, on site – the typical resident was a middle manager on a six-month course. The need for flexibility drove the plan – a 'tartan' grid superimposed on a central spine containing teaching and communal spaces, with residential accommodation around the perimeter. Frank Newby devised a structural system with internal junctions marked by four column units, which provided routes for services and solved the problem of the low bearing pressure of the site. In section, the buildings respond to the sloping site, with an enclosed bridge spanning a central court to provide access to the residential blocks. The study bedrooms in the earlier phases of the development

above: Exterior of the Oxford Centre for Management Studies showing the entrance sequence

are arranged on two levels, with a sleeping space above a well-equipped study area and sloping glazing providing attractive daylit spaces for private study. The original library was at the heart of the college, toplit and surrounded by teaching and office spaces on two levels. Externally, zinc was used as a low-maintenance cladding material – there had been problems with the lead cladding at Brasenose. Richard Burton convinced the client of the suitability of the material – 'the whole of Paris is roofed in zinc', he commented. The design strategy served the institution well, adapting easily to changing accommodation needs as the college grew and developed its teaching programme. Its success reflects ABK's commitment to making buildings which address a broader agenda than the purely practical – what Richard Burton defines as 'the group of elements which bridge between the utilitarian and the higher aspects of man'.[4]

Two features of the business school that were to characterise so much of ABK's subsequent work were the emphasis on integrating art and craftsmanship into the buildings (with furniture by John Makepeace and Fred Baier, and a notable collection of art works) and collaboration – the first of many – with landscape architect James Hope (who had worked on the Cummins factory and was later to work at St Mary's Hospital) to produce what Burton describes as 'a water garden running through the courtyards of the buildings'. In 2008 Templeton College merged with Green College, and the Kennington site was transferred into the ownership of Oxford University's Said Business School.

above: Interior of the library at the Oxford Centre for Management Studies
opposite: Courtyard with planting by James Hope

Keble College

The early phases of the Templeton project overlapped with the first phase of ABK's
additions to Keble College, Oxford, another project led by Peter Ahrends, the result of a
competitive interview process held in 1969. The commission was for a very substantial
addition to the college, the first since William Butterfield's collegiate buildings had been
completed in 1882, to provide additional residential accommodation. The long L-shaped
site, along Blackhall Road and Museum Road, was occupied by a line of Victorian semi-
detached houses owned by the college. Significantly, ABK's first instinct was to retain
these houses, refurbish them as student accommodation, infill the gaps between them
and create a new glazed link at the rear, addressing the existing college buildings and
containing a common room, bar and other facilities. Keble was, however, anxious to
commission a new building which would be the equal of those completed or under
construction for other colleges – 'they wanted to make a statement', says Ahrends.

The project was realised in two main phases the first completed in 1973 and the second
in 1977. The first, on the southern edge of the site, contained 64 student rooms, plus 12
rooms for fellows; the second phase provided a further 26 student rooms and two flats for
academics, plus a new student bar and middle common room. The architects' first instinct
was to give the new building its own entrance and to open it up to the city, but the college
wanted to retain a single entrance to the site and shied away from the idea of openness.
The new building was consequently conceived as a 'wall', one room deep, each room

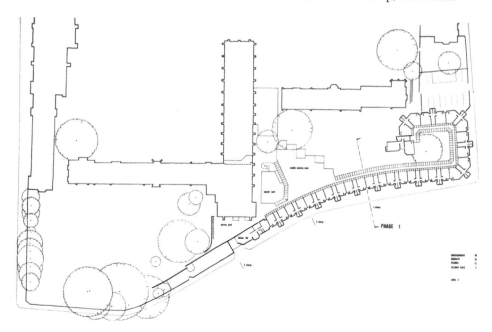

above: **Plan of ABK's residential building at Keble College**

having views out to the street and into the heart of the college. To the street it is faced
in brick, with service towers (housing bathrooms) and narrow slit windows giving it a
strongly defensive look. Brick was an obvious material to use at Keble, but it is not the red
brick favoured by Butterfield but a buff brick not dissimilar to that used at the university
chaplaincy. 'We couldn't compete with Butterfield's polychromy – the brick we used was
suggested by Richard', says Ahrends.

ABK's Keble project, like Powell & Moya's work at Brasenose and other post-war
additions to Oxbridge colleges, had to address the issue of ingrained traditions.
Butterfield had, in fact, dispensed with one Oxford tradition at Keble, substituting
corridors for staircases as a means of access to the student rooms. ABK reinstated
the traditional arrangement. The first phase of the development was formed as a
small quad, another traditional form, with a sinuous curve of rooms then extending
northwards along Blackhall Road and stepping down from four storeys to one at its
northern end in order to provide a good view of the gable end of Butterfield's dining
hall. (The curve was to be a feature of a number of subsequent ABK projects run by
Peter Ahrends – this was its first appearance in the firm's work.) On the inside, the
building is entirely faced in tinted glass with a walkway providing access to the staircases – the aesthetic is that of James Stirling's Florey Building at Queen's College,

above: **The exterior of the Keble College building – brick-faced and presenting a defensive front to the street**

top: The internal 'street' at Keble College, with student bar
above: Student room at Keble College, Oxford

completed in 1971, a project that clearly had some influence on ABK's designs, which retain their radical edge 40 years on. Writing of the first phase of development, Mark Girouard, in a generally favourable review which particularly applauded the relationship of the glazed inner façade to the Butterfield buildings, felt that 'the building leaves one with a slightly uneasy feeling that it is putting on an act when an act, however brilliant, wasn't called for'.[5] A later critic argued that 'nowhere in Oxford is the language of modernism used with more subtlety'.[6] ABK's work at Keble was listed at Grade II* in 1999 – but this did not prevent a section of the building, deliberately kept low to protect views of Butterfield's hall, from being demolished for a new block designed by Rick Mather.

Further Work in Dublin: Trinity and St Andrew's Colleges

ABK's relationship with Trinity College, Dublin, remained close after the completion of the Berkeley Library and was the foundation of the practice's establishing itself as a major presence on the Irish scene. A year after the opening of the library, ABK, under Paul Koralek and Patrick Stubbings (who became a partner in 1974), was commissioned (following a competition in which Powell & Moya and the leading Irish practice of Scott Tallon Walker were initially shortlisted) to design a very large new building for the college, providing teaching facilities for the arts, economics and social-studies faculties.

The site was in the Fellows' Garden, close to Nassau Street, where ABK formed a new entrance to the college, a radical move indicating the increasing integration of Trinity into the life of the city. Enclosed to the east by the Berkeley Library and to the north by the Great Library, the garden was refashioned as Fellows' Square, a continuation of the historic pattern of development at Trinity. The brief included the provision of a new undergraduate library (the Lecky Library), a capacious 400-seat auditorium ideal for public lectures, an art gallery and social spaces, but most of the building was to be given over to lecture theatres and seminar rooms and a large number of studies for academics. The challenge was to create a building which would be at home in its context – its height restricted to that of neighbouring buildings – and which would be internally legible and enjoyable despite its size. Necessarily, given the constraints on height, the new Arts Building (finally completed in 1979) had a deep plan but its stepped form reduced its impact on the new square, while the extensive use of glazing on the (north) elevation addressing the square further ameliorated its apparent scale. In contrast, wrote John Winter in the *Architects' Journal*, the façade to Nassau Street was 'both forbidding and apparently random', though it had the practical benefit of excluding traffic noise.[7] (The same strategy of creating a defensive wall to the street had been applied at Keble.) But, as Paul Koralek points out, the principle of a new entrance to the college, allowing the public to walk through the site, was itself a radical departure – Trinity had traditionally kept itself apart from the city behind its high walls. The 'hole in the wall' on Nassau Street symbolised the end of the college's isolation as a Protestant enclave in a Catholic country. Even more significant was the fact that the project (which had generated some contro-

top: The Arts Faculty building at Trinity College, Dublin, occupying a site in the former Fellows' Garden
above: Interior of the library in the Trinity College Arts Faculty

versy and fierce criticism from conservation bodies) was entirely funded by the Irish Government, reflecting Trinity's integration into the national education system as part of the National University of Ireland.

In such a large (16,700 square metres/180,000 square feet) and tightly planned building, including both communal and public spaces and private teaching and study accommodation over five floors, it was necessary to establish a hierarchy of spaces, 'to give a sense of the whole and yet at the same time to create variety and a sense of individuality and intimacy for the people using the building'. Externally, there is a clear expression of the activities it houses: the auditorium and lecture theatres are clad in granite, the library has a fully glazed elevation facing Fellows' Square and the faculty accommodation on the top three floors is contained within the expressed concrete frame. A series of open courts provides daylight and a sense of openness to those occupying these levels. But the key feature of the building is the main concourse, extending over the two lower levels, with a café, which is a busy social focus for the college, and access to lecture theatres, library and the Douglas Hyde art gallery. Soon after its opening, the concourse was 'constantly frequented, both by alumni and by shop- and office-workers from the other side of Nassau Street'.[8] In effect, it shifted the centre of gravity of the college and helped open it up to the city.

above: **The Arts Faculty Building adjacent to the back of the Berkeley Library (on the right)**

'TCD' remained a loyal client of the practice as ABK expanded its workload in an increasingly buoyant Ireland from 1990 onwards – in 1991 it opened an office in Dublin, initially led by Paul de Freine, which was to benefit from the booming years of the 'tiger economy'. The Dublin office was set up, initially very much as a 'pied-à-terre', after ABK was commissioned in 1991 to renovate and extend the dental hospital attached to Trinity College's medical faculty. The Victorian hospital was located in a far corner of the campus, beyond the playing fields and science faculty buildings. The prime mover in the development project was the head of the dental school, Professor Derry Shanley, who admired ABK's earlier work for the college and had been much impressed by the new John Lewis store in Kingston-upon-Thames. Shanley drew up the brief for the project and proved an exemplary client. ABK's designs responded to the architecture of the old hospital, with a curved façade of brick on the street frontage mediating between Victorian and modern – the elevation of the new building which faces into the campus is frankly contemporary in manner, with a slender glazed tower as a marker. The new wing contains the clinical facilities, with the treatment areas laid out on a triangular module which creates more intimate spaces for treating patients. The refurbished Victorian block contains lecture rooms and staff offices. The two buildings are linked by an impressive atrium, used to display an interesting collection of art works. The dental hospital opened in 1998. In the

above: The addition to the Dublin Dental Hospital defers to the red-brick and terracotta façade of the Victorian hospital
opposite: Internal atrium at the Dublin Dental Hospital, connecting the original building with ABK's extension

following year, Trinity commissioned ABK to design an extension to the Arts Building. The scheme, on which Paul Koralek worked with Paul de Freine and Robert Davys (who had come to Dublin after working on the Moscow Embassy), created a lightweight top-floor addition to the building under a series of curved roofs. It was a considerable disappointment nonetheless when ABK lost out to the Irish practice McCullough Mulvin in the competition to extend the Berkeley Library.

Educational projects were to figure prominently in ABK's workload in Ireland. St Andrew's College, Booterstown, in the Dublin suburbs, was completed in 1972, an entirely new co-educational school with junior and secondary departments on the same site and provision for boarders as well as day pupils. Externally austere, the low-rise building is planned around two parallel routes flanking a central multipurpose hall. Teaching spaces are pleasingly varied in character and garden courts introduce light into the heart of the complex.

above: The multipurpose central hall at St Andrew's College, Booterstown

UK School Design

ABK had come too late on the scene to benefit from the British school-building boom of the late 1940s and 1950s, but Eastfield Primary School in Leicestershire, completed in 1968, incorporated ideas later developed at Booterstown. The idea, developed in discussion with the county's head of education, Stewart Mason, was to break down the

above: **Informal spaces at Eastfield Primary School at Thurmaston in Leicestershire provided a contrast to traditional compartmentalisation**

traditional compartmentalisation of schools, move away from the idea of the class as a self-contained unit, and create a series of spaces varied in size and character around a central courtyard. Quiet rooms provided a place to which children could 'escape' when they felt the need. A significant innovation in terms of school design in Leicestershire was the principle of 'a percentage for art' – to become a theme of ABK's work – with the commissioning of a sculpture by Norman Dilworth. Writing to Paul Koralek in 1985, the then headmaster commented that the school was 'strikingly light, open and cheerful' – visitors 'have difficulty in believing that it was opened as long ago as 1968'. This was a project which rethought the whole nature and purpose of a school, just as ABK's new public library at Redcar in the north-east of England redefined the idea of a library as a community building.

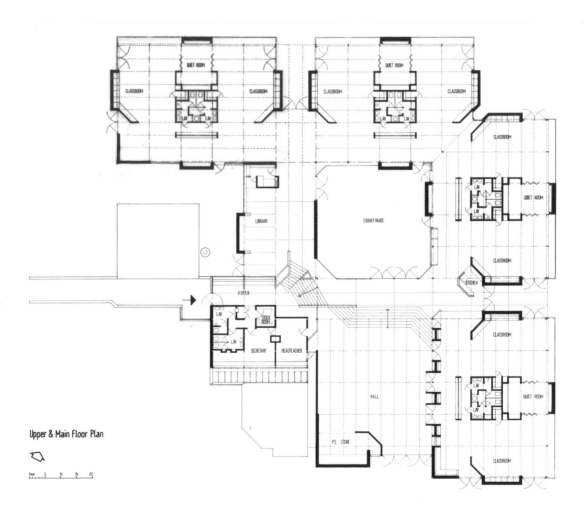

Upper & Main Floor Plan

above: The plan of Eastfield School revolved around a central courtyard

Redcar Library

Redcar was the product of a new campaign of public library construction in which Norman Reuter, an architect working for the Department of Education and Science, played a leading role. The commission came in 1966. ABK's Berkeley Library was already nearing completion, but the needs of the people of an industrial town were very different from those of university students and academics. Reuter believed that 'the library should never be considered as a monument or as a cultural retreat; but as a source of pleasure, recreation, information, and learning; readily available to all'.[9] ABK, with Peter Ahrends and subsequently Richard Burton as partner in charge, assisted by David Castle, took up Reuter's brief with enthusiasm. A novel addition to the range of facilities proposed was a café. It was also proposed to construct a small theatre as part of the scheme, but subsequent economies ruled this out. The library was completed and opened early in 1971.

The plan of Redcar Library reflects the idea of openness and accessibility, with the ground floor housing the lending and children's libraries and coffee shop conceived as an open-plan, largely single-storey space. A vivid orange carpet extending across the

above: The interior of Redcar Library, a rigorous design using a steel frame and making excellent use of natural light

whole space was a talking point – this was probably the first use of carpet in a public library and gave the interior an almost domestic character. The reference library, along with a lecture hall and meeting rooms, was elevated at first-floor level on the western edge of the site – a balcony provided views down into the ground floor. In terms of materials too, Redcar was a radical new departure for ABK. Instead of the weighty concrete structure of Berkeley Library, a steel frame was used – Redcar was a steel town and most of the (standardised) components were locally made. The steel frame was boldly exposed inside the building; externally, the roof, clad in corrugated steel sheeting, was striking in form, its serrated profile incorporating angled rooflights which provided effective controlled daylight. Furniture designed by the architects, including steel-framed shelving units, reinforced the rigorous aesthetic of lightness and light. The *Architectural Review* commented that the interior of the library 'looks neither like a factory nor like a house. It is essentially a large open public space – were it not for the books on the shelves it could be used for many purposes'.[10] In a critique which placed Redcar in the context of new library design, Michael Brawne praised the 'exuberance and occasional playfulness' with which steel was used in the building, but argued that 'the real opportunities, one feels, are still to come at Redcar'.[11] The library would come into its own, he suggested, when plans for a series of public buildings on adjacent land were realised. Sadly, this vision was not realised and by 2011 the building was disused. Following a ministerial decision to reject English Heritage's strong recommendation that the library be listed, it was demolished in the autumn of 2011.

Maidenhead Library

The loss of the library was all the more regrettable since ABK's other public library, at Maidenhead, had been listed in 2003. Completed in 1972, Maidenhead Library was, like Redcar, a building which embodied new thinking about the public library as a resource for the whole community. It was planned as a series of integrated spaces under a great roof, a clear-span steel space frame assembled on the ground and jacked into position in a single day to rest on eight cruciform concrete columns. Beneath the roof, lending library, children's library, music library and exhibition space are located at ground level. The reference library is on an upper level, conceived as an open gallery rather than an enclosed space. The contours of the site made it possible to place book stacks and administrative space in a semi-basement. Brick was used extensively as a cladding material on the concrete structure, both externally and internally. The retention of a venerable cedar tree was part of the brief for the scheme, a marker on a heavily used pedestrian route across the town centre. Superficially, Maidenhead, with Paul Koralek leading the ABK team, lacked the radical edge of Redcar. Perhaps its location, in a prosperous Home Counties town, dictated a degree of decorum. But Lance Wright, writing in the *Architectural Review*, considered the library 'a startling building ...

opposite: **Exterior of Redcar Library – demolished in 2011**

because it realises in a very categorical and complete way one of the constituent
dreams of the Modern Movement: the dream of separating walls from roof, thus of
constructing "a building inside a building"; the dream of placing a sculptured form
which is free to bulge outwards or to indent as use requires, inside a translucent shell'.[12]
Still in full use, the Maidenhead library wears its radicalism lightly.

Portsmouth Polytechnic Library

Redcar and Maidenhead, as well as the Berkeley Library, fed into ABK's programme
for the new library at Portsmouth Polytechnic (now University). The practice had
been commissioned to prepare a master plan for a site at Ravelin House, where open
parkland provided scope for a new campus to be developed, bringing together departments scattered in a variety of buildings across the centre of Portsmouth. The master
plan (published in 1973), providing for a series of residential and teaching buildings to
be constructed along two sides of the triangular site over the next decade, was shelved
as spending cuts in the dire financial climate of the mid-1970s slashed expenditure on

above: Interior of Maidenhead Library, showing the steel space-frame roof enclosing a variety of internal
spaces
opposite: Exterior of Maidenhead Library

top: Perspective of the interior of the library at Portsmouth Polytechnic
above: The exterior of the library at Portsmouth Polytechnic, the only completed element of a masterplan for what became Portsmouth University
opposite: Interior of the library at Portsmouth, featuring a stepped section and a lightweight glazed roof

higher education. However, the first phase of the new library was given the go-ahead and construction began in 1975, with the library opened in September 1977. ABK was commissioned to design a second, smaller phase in 1986.

The starting point for the development of the project was the extremely modest budget – in comparison with the Berkeley Library, this was to be a very economical building. It would have formed the northern termination of a long teaching block for the arts and social-sciences faculties, its stepped form echoing that of the Arts Building at Trinity College. Some adjustments to the designs for the library were required since, with the rest of the project cancelled, it would now be a one-off building, arbitrarily detached from the complex of which it was to form part. The library, accommodating 500 readers, was planned across three levels on a stepped section – a feature which became something of an ABK trademark – under a sweeping glazed roof constructed of plywood panels supported on lightweight steel trusses. Reflectors channelled light into the building. Stairs and lifts to the upper floors were conceived as freestanding towers within the open interior. The in-situ concrete structure of the building was freely exposed inside. Paul Koralek wrote that 'the library is conceived as a workshop for study. Its character and appearance are the result of a direct expression of the various components of its construction. All structural and servicing elements are exposed and carefully designed to relate to each other in an ordered way. The building therefore reveals its nature in a very direct way'.[13] The depth of the plan, in fact, made it impossible for the interior to be entirely naturally ventilated – ventilation ducts were a prominent feature of the spaces beneath the floor slabs. Within the constraints of the brief and budget there was a serious attempt to create something of the intimacy of the Dublin library, but the small, quiet study areas found in the latter could not be created in the context of the severe pressure on space at Portsmouth. An architecture student at the polytechnic commented: 'the interior is overcrowded, almost garrulous'. In summer, there were problems of overheating, while the ventilation system was noisy. None of this was really the fault of the architects of what was a 'very exciting' building – the problem was that it was just part of an incomplete project.[14]

Hooke Park

The Portsmouth library was designed at a time when thinking about the environmental impact of building services was in transition – Alex Gordon, as President of the RIBA, had coined the phrase 'long life/low energy/loose fit' in 1972 as a recipe for the architecture of the future. The oil crisis of 1973 was a major catalyst for change. ABK had always been to the fore in terms of environmental thinking – the Northlands housing at Basildon, the W. H. Smith offices at Swindon, and the Cummins engine factory had all been progressive in this respect. However, the early 1980s saw the practice working on a project which was a radical statement about the use of natural resources, and on which Richard Burton worked with an inspirational team and for a visionary client, the

furniture designer and maker John Makepeace. In 1977, Makepeace, who ran a school of furniture design at Parnham House in Dorset, had founded the Parnham Trust as an educational charity concerned with the sustainable use of timber. In 1982, the Trust acquired 350 acres (146 hectares) of woodland at Hooke Park, close to Parnham, with the idea of establishing a base there with workshops and residential accommodation for students. Makepeace approached the eminent German engineer and architect Frei Otto, the world's leading authority on tensile and membrane structures, for advice, the

above: The residential building at Hooke Park, constructed in 1985 using softwood thinning from the surrounding woodlands

idea being to construct the buildings at Hooke Park from material available on site, notably the thinnings – the timber thinned out from a commercial woodland to make space for the main crop of trees to grow. At Frei Otto's suggestion, Richard Burton was brought in as co-designer, soon joined by Buro Happold, under Ted Happold and Michael Dickson, as consultant structural and services engineers. The team worked on a master plan for the site – 'our mission turned out to be no less than the development of a system of design and construction for the use of "waste wood"', Burton recalls. In effect, the challenge was to design a new system of building construction using a previously disregarded material which had in the past been used for nothing more substantial than fencing – much was burnt as firewood. The development of a method of jointing the timber was a key issue and the subject of research at Buro Happold – the use of epoxy resin as a jointing medium was probably inspired by Ted Happold's experience at NASA.

The first building completed at Hooke Park – very much a prototype – was a house containing staff accommodation, constructed in the very wet summer of 1985 with William Moorwood of ABK acting as full-time site architect, liaising with a local carpentry firm, Dowding & Udall. The house was constructed of softwood thinnings at a cost of £50,000. The 600 square metre (6,500 square foot) workshop building followed,

above: **Exterior of the workshop building at Hooke Park**

a much more substantial structure, formed of three timber shells covered in a heavily insulated double-skin PVC membrane roof. The result is a building which is internally impressive, with something of the spatial quality of a traditional rustic barn. Barns were, however, heavyweight structures. The Hooke workshop is extremely lightweight, with end walls filled with glass and plastic panels (using Makrolon®, a double-skinned translucent plastic also used for the rooflight extending the length of the building). Internally, the western bay of the building housed an office on an upper-level platform, producing what critic Peter Davey described as 'a rather Wild West appearance'. Davey described the project as 'a continuous experiment', predicting that 'Hooke may be the start of a revolution in timber construction which will have incalculable beneficial consequences'.[15] Later development at Hooke Park included a student residence designed, using similar technology to that of ABK's buildings, by Edward Cullinan Architects. The eventual winding-up of the Parnham Trust led to concerns about the future of Hooke Park. However, with considerable input from Richard Burton the site was transferred in 2003 into the ownership of the Architectural Association. It has been intensively used since then by students from the AA, and Burton has been closely involved in the development of a master plan for the future development of the site and the AA courses based there.

above: Interior of the workshop building at Hooke Park in Dorset, a pioneering and sophisticated example of 'green' architecture

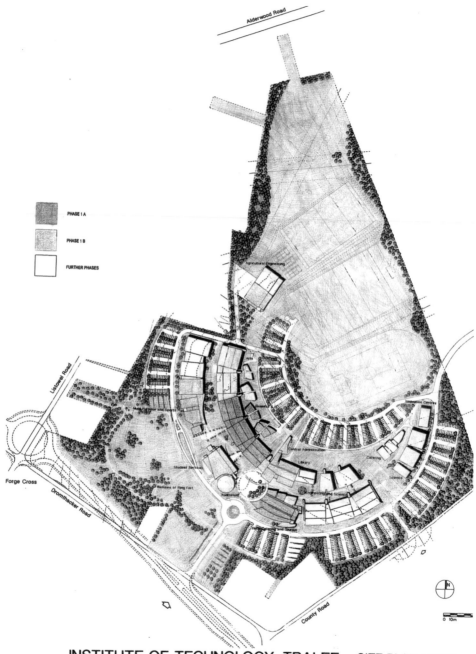

INSTITUTE OF TECHNOLOGY, TRALEE   SITE PLAN 1:2500

above: Plan of the new campus for the Tralee Institute

Educational Work in Ireland and Scotland

ABK's Dublin office was responsible for much of the practice's work from the mid-1990s on, and was eventually to be established, under the leadership of partners Robert Davys and John Parker, as a separate practice, developing its own distinctive approach to design. The Tralee Institute of Technology was ABK's first Irish project following the establishment of the Dublin office in the early 1990s. Its curved form makes excellent use of the dramatic site. The Institute of Technology at Blanchardstown, outside Dublin, an institution delivering training and education from apprentice to degree level and linked to a major business-park development promoted by the Irish Development Agency, has echoes of earlier ABK projects. The first phase of development was completed in 2002. Peter Ahrends led the design team, and the curving, sculptural form of the buildings betrays his touch. The use of angled columns supporting a curved roof on the student centre/sports hall block and corrugated aluminium cladding recall Ahrends' Cummins factory, completed in 1983. Ahrends found working in Ireland enjoyable: 'it's more radical', he said, 'there is an acceptance that, as an architect, you have a voice in the making of contemporary culture'.[16]

above: The new Tralee Institute of Technology was one of several major Irish projects by ABK in the 1990s

Back in New Labour Britain, ABK had to contend with a political climate in which the Private Finance Initiative (PFI) and the use of design-and-build contracts disempowered the architect. Nonetheless, ABK's John Wheatley College in the East End of Glasgow was, though a design-and-build project, a building which bore the stamp of the partnership. The central concourse, triangular in form and roofed with air-filled ETFE cushions, provided a social space acting as a gateway to three blocks of accommodation, housing respectively teaching space, administration and workshops. The central atrium/concourse became a commonplace of school design in the years of Building Schools for the Future, but in this instance the architects could justly claim that the quest for democratic, flexible space was one that had been pursued in their educational projects over nearly half a century.

above: The bold aesthetic of the Blanchardstown Institute of Technology

Notes

1   Alan Colquhoun, 'Library, Trinity College, Dublin', *Architectural Review*, October 1967, p.265.

2   Dan Cruickshank, 'Berkeley Library, Trinity College, Dublin 1967–1997', *RIBA Journal*, October 1997, p.75.

3   Elain Harwood, 'Early work' in Kenneth Powell (ed.), *Collaborations: the architecture of ABK*, London, August/Birkhäuser, 2002, p.48.

4   Richard Burton, 'Architecture – towards an holistic approach' in *Ahrends Burton and Koralek*, London, Academy Editions, 1991, p. 25.

5   Mark Girouard, 'Residential Building, Keble College, Oxford', *Architectural Review*, July 1973, p.12.

6   Geoffrey Tyack, *Oxford: an architectural guide*, Oxford, Oxford University Press, 1998, p.325.

7   John Winter, 'Arts Faculty building, Trinity College, Dublin', *Architects' Journal*, 18 July 1979, p.127.

8   Lance Wright, 'Arts Faculty, Trinity College Dublin', *Architectural Review*, July 1979, p.43.

9   Cited in English Heritage listing advice report, 30 March 2011, p.1.

10 Michael Brawne,'ABK Redcar', *Architectural Review*, July 1971, p.48.

11 ibid., pp.53–4.

12 Lance Wright, 'Library, Maidenhead, Berkshire', *Architectural Review*, May 1974, p.267.

13 *Architects' Journal*, 4 April 1979, p.689.

14 ibid., pp.691–3.

15 Peter Davey, 'Forest commission', *Architectural Review*, September 1990, pp.47–8.

16 Peter Ahrends quoted in Frank Macdonald, 'Ireland' in Kenneth Powell (ed.), *Collaborations: the architecture of ABK,* London, August/Birkhäuser, 2002, p.137.

3   Housing and Some Houses

Their practice up and running and with fees coming in, the founding partners of ABK put down roots in London. Peter Ahrends and Paul Koralek still live in the early nineteenth-century houses, a few hundred yards apart in a quiet street in Kentish Town, where they raised their families within walking distance of the office in Chalcot Road, NW1, to which ABK moved in the late 1960s. Richard Burton and his wife Mireille continued to live in a house of similar vintage in St John's Wood, rented from the Eyre Estate, from the time of their marriage in 1956 until 1979. They then moved to a house close to Kentish Town tube station – it was there that Burton planned the new house a few yards away which has been his home for over 20 years: 'a country house in the city', as he describes it.

The modern house in Britain had acquired a respectable lineage by the 1950s. Even in the 1930s, the fashion for 'white Modern' had receded in favour of a 'self referential and educated type of Modernism' in which a richer palette of materials, notably timber, reflected a desire to integrate architecture and landscape.[1] The New Empiricism of the immediate post-war years equally signalled a move away from the universalism of the International Style. Ahrends, Burton and Koralek, studying at the AA in the 1950s, were less enraptured by Le Corbusier than others of their generation and the practice's first house, the Bryan Brown house in Devon, completed in 1964, is an early example of ABK's alternative, naturalistic Modernism, and reflects the influence of Wright. Naturalism and response to context were to be central to later ABK houses, in locations as diverse as the Irish countryside and the Old City of Jerusalem.

Headington Houses

Some of the ideas which were to emerge in its housing projects were seen in the group of five houses at Old Headington, just outside Oxford, completed in 1969. The client for the development was the Lower Farm Housing Group, a group of Oxford academics assembled by the medieval historian (and Fellow of Queen's College) John Prestwich and his wife, and fellow historian, Menna, who taught at St Hilda's College. John Prestwich had come across ABK when he was one of the panel interviewing prospective architects for the college's Florey Building – the commission went to James Stirling, but Prestwich (a Lancastrian who came from a family of architects and surveyors) had been

opposite: The houses at Dunstan Road, Headington, Oxford, embodied ideas about the balance between privacy and community

impressed by ABK and approached the practice as possible architect for the Headington houses. The project married the ideals of community and privacy, with each house given a private walled garden and, north of the houses, a continuous wall, incorporating garages, screening them from the street and unifying them as a group. It is tempting to see in this scheme the influence of Serge Chermayeff and Christopher Alexander's *Community and Privacy*, which first appeared in 1963 and was to transform ideas about mass housing. Constructed of concrete block to a modest budget, the five houses were simply detailed and designed to be adaptable as the needs of the residents changed over the years. A later resident was Norman Leyland, sometime Bursar of Brasenose College and founding Director of the Oxford Centre for Management Studies, for which ABK was the architectural firm.

Basildon New Town: Chalvedon, Felmore and Whitmore Court Housing

ABK's long association with Basildon New Town in Essex began with a planning study for the south-west area of the town, where around 20,000 new homes were envisaged, and moved on to a commission from Basildon's Chief Architect/Planner Douglas Galloway to design 1,360 dwellings, housing around 5,000 people, in the Chalvedon area of the expanding town. Chermayeff's and Alexander's thinking, Richard Burton concedes, certainly influenced the development of this project – securing it was a major

above: The Headington houses were built for five academic families, led by John and Menna Prestwich

achievement for a practice which had built just six houses. Phased construction began
in 1973 and extended over the next four years. By the late 1960s, the fashion for high-rise
social housing had receded – by the early 1970s, medium- and subsequently low-rise
projects became the norm. Concerns which had not been to the fore a decade earlier
– sustainability and the need to foster community life – began to be taken seriously.
ABK had never been attracted to the idea of high-rise living, and on cost grounds alone
there was no case for building high in Basildon. Richard Burton says of the Chalvedon
housing: 'there was no attempt at originality – the idea was to create a habitable place
planned around a series of gardens and pedestrian routes'. The formula was that used
successfully by Phippen Randall & Parkes for their housing at The Ryde, Hatfield,
completed in 1966. The latter project was single storey; at Chalvedon, ABK added
two-storey houses and three-storey maisonettes to the mix.

The 33-hectare (80-acre) site at Chalvedon was unremarkable in its topography:
mostly flat, scrubby and with few established trees. The decision to build no more than
three storeys high, using traditional construction techniques in brick and timber, was
taken at the very beginning of the project and was to establish the basic philosophy
underpinning ABK's subsequent housing schemes. A major innovation in the development of the project was the decision, taken while the first phase of construction
was under way, to enlist the services of a social psychologist, Peter Ellis of the London
School of Economics (LSE), to research the views of the residents on the new housing
and to incorporate his findings into the later phases of development. Mireille Burton

above: **Section through a typical housing unit at Chalvedon, Basildon**

above: The housing at Chalvedon was designed to foster a sense of community and offered an alternative to discredited high-rise housing projects

FELMORE ONE HOUSING

assisted Ellis with a series of interviews. This move was in tune with the recommenda-
tions of the 1969 Skeffington Report, commissioned by the then Ministry of Housing
and Local Government, which had called for greater public involvement in the planning
process. Even as the first houses were going up, the architects were establishing links
with local residents and seeking their views on the success of the designs. Peter Ellis
worked with ABK over a period of three years (1975–7).

The development was popular with residents from the beginning, partly because
it seemed to have a sense of community. Ellis concluded that its architecture was an
equally important factor:

> many give as their reasons that 'it doesn't look like a council estate'. The
> architecture belongs to a genre which is associated with private housing. Its
> inhabitants perceive it as less institutionalised than traditional 'estates'.
> The importance of the design in this context lies not in the actual physical
> configuration and its immediate impact on the senses but in the kind of life
> style which it represents.[2]

The look of the houses, comparable to that of the private-sector developments
designed by Eric Lyons for Span, was a contributory factor to this positive response

above: **Plan of ABK's second large housing project for Basildon, at Felmore**

but the friendliness of the layout, which typically grouped 60 dwellings around large communal gardens, was another element in its success. As early as 1957, Michael Young and Peter Willmott had analysed the disintegration of communities bodily transplanted from the East End of London to new out-of-town estates in *Family and Kinship in East London*. Ellis concluded that 'architects cannot create community, but they *can* provide the physical potential for it, and this, to a large extent, ABK have done at Chalvedon'.[3]

Among the changes made in phase 3 of the development on the basis of Ellis's findings were redesigned entrance arrangements to some of the houses, resolving a perceived confusion between 'front' and 'back', and a move away from expensive all-electric heating systems. The research fed into the design of the Chalvedon Centre, with its community hall, supermarket and shops. In a detailed architectural critique of the scheme, Richard MacCormac concluded that Chalvedon's apparent success was, like that of Span in the private housing market, that of 'an aesthetic idea which prevails over objectives of a lower order'. Residents were prepared to accept terraced rather than semi-detached houses, the lack of garages, and small private gardens because they warmed to the overall environment of the place. MacCormac continued: 'perhaps the degree to which public housing can succeed at this level will depend on a change in

above: **Extensive planting contributed to the success of the Felmore housing, which was also pioneering in its low-energy strategy**

housing policy which will end both its distinct and arbitrarily lower social status and the public tenant's passive role, allowing the form of his house to express his style. ABK have gone as far towards this goal as the present system allows.'[4]

ABK's strategy at Chalvedon, social as much as architectural, along with that of Ralph Erskine in the 'Byker Wall' housing project (which went on site in 1971 and was admired by ABK), prefigured much of the thinking of the community architecture movement that became an influential force in Britain in the 1980s. Richard Burton argues that 'our methods changed the course of how architects work with clients'. The success of Chalvedon led, in 1974, to a further commission to ABK, under Burton, assisted by Christine Price, for 418 houses in the Felmore area of the town. The Felmore scheme, again commissioned by Douglas Galloway and with his assistant Clive Plumb actively involved, was completed in 1980. It saw many of the key ideas behind Chalvedon revisited: one- and two-storey terraced houses, built of brick and timber, arranged in groups, with areas of public open space separating them. But what was novel about Felmore was the new emphasis on energy issues – this was the first major housing project in Britain to embody such an extensive range of energy-conserving strategies. A central power plant (fuelled at first by coal, later by gas) provided each housing group with efficient district heating. The ducts for the heating were incorporated into covered walkways linking the terraces. Good insulation and overhanging eaves to baffle solar gain contributed to the energy-saving potential of the scheme – 30/40 per cent over conventional housing. Aesthetically, Felmore, Burton acknowledges, is shame-lessly picturesque – even the power plants, with their gaily painted flues, are made into objects of visual delight.

The energy studies for Felmore fed into other ABK projects, including the W. H. Smith offices and St Mary's Hospital as well as the 1981 low-energy Abbey National housing design project. The low-energy agenda of Felmore was further developed in the plans for housing at Valescure in southern France, on which Richard Burton collabo-rated with Kate Mackintosh. The scheme was for housing, hotel and other leisure facilities picturesquely grouped on a wooded site. It remained unbuilt. ABK's third Basildon housing project, Whitmore Court – a previous project for student housing on the site having been abandoned – was taken in hand by Richard Burton's team. The brief was to design a dense development providing housing for single people and for the aged (who were provided with a day centre and resident warden). The scheme eschews the picturesqueness of Chalvedon and Felmore in favour of a tougher aesthetic of brick and precast concrete, with flats in five blocks enclosing landscaped gardens.

Collen House, Wicklow

ABK's close relationship with Ireland produced one outstanding domestic project. Lyall Collen was a graduate of Trinity College, a very successful industrialist and a great supporter of the library project. A Protestant by religion, he was the driving force behind the establishment of St Andrew's College, Booterstown, backing ABK's

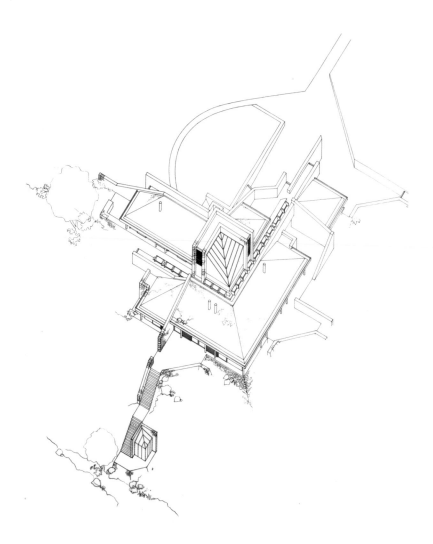

innovative proposals for the school. Paul Koralek describes Collen as 'one of our great collaborators'. It was for Collen and his family that Koralek designed the house at Glencree in County Wicklow which so clearly restates the practice's concern for merging architecture and landscape. The steeply sloping site (just 32 kilometres/20 miles from the centre of Dublin) is sublime, with views across mountains and moors. The house, built by the client's own construction company, is inserted into the landscape, its L-shaped plan angled to take maximum advantage of views to the south.

above: Isometric of the Collen House in County Wicklow, one of Ireland's finest modern houses
opposite: The major remodelling of the Collen House begun in 2003 included a double-height living space, replacing an existing staircase

Planted roofs and the use of local stone for external walls are part of the response to context. The house epitomised the modernising mood of Ireland in the 1970s. In 2003, however, ABK was commissioned to refurbish and extend the house, bringing it into line with changing family needs and up-to-date ideas of comfortable living. The plan was extended to create a new master-bedroom suite at the end of one wing (the former master bedroom became a bathroom) and a new kitchen, dining room and family room to terminate the other. The approach to the house was also modified, not least to create a larger turning area for vehicles. A new main stair was inserted to provide a stronger connection between the main level of the house and the upper level, which had originally been designed as a self-contained flat. Windows were replaced using aluminium frames, and were generally enlarged. Services were upgraded in line with an increased concern for sustainability – underfloor heating was provided by a heat pump powered by the nearby river.

above: The Collen House is an excellent example of ABK's ability to build in sympathy with the landscape as remodelled in 2003

Nebenzahl House, Jerusalem

ABK had found another remarkable client in Yitzhak Ernst Nebenzahl (1907–92),
who, as State Comptroller of Israel, was effectively second in rank only to the
country's president. German-born Nebenzahl, who had made his fortune in the paper
industry, was an Orthodox Jew. Following the Six Day War of 1967, when Israeli forces
comprehensively routed those of Egypt, Syria and Jordan, East Jerusalem, including
the Old City, was annexed by Israel after nearly 20 years of Jordanian rule. Nebenzahl
wanted to play his part in regenerating the Jewish Quarter of the Old City post-1967 as
part of the Israeli capital. The Jewish background of ABK's founding partners doubtless
played a part in the practice's appointment to design a new house for Nebenzahl and
his family on a site just inside the Old City, with views right across Jerusalem to the
Dome of the Rock, the Temple Mount and Mount of Olives. Paul Koralek was the lead
partner for the project, with significant input from Peter Ahrends and Richard Burton.
ABK (recommended by a former employee, now based in Israel) had been telephoned by
Nebenzahl in the summer of 1968 with an invitation to come to Jerusalem and discuss
the house project. By February 1969 the designs were finalised, and the house was built
in 1970–3.

The new house followed the lines of an existing group of buildings, along the line
of the ancient city wall – strict planning laws demanded that all external surfaces be
of stone. The house actually contained three separate apartments: the top floor for
Nebenzahl and his wife, the lower floors for members of his family. A guest flat was

above: Sketch by Richard Burton showing the site of the Nebenzahl House close to the ancient city walls of
Jerusalem

provided on the ground floor. The designs were carefully vetted to ensure that they accorded with Old Testament prescriptions – for example, no floor could overhang a street and a kosher kitchen was provided. They took advantage of the magnificent site, with window openings concentrated on the eastern elevation of the house where they afforded fine views from the Old City. A series of photographs taken during the construction process (still using traditional timber scaffolding) records what Koralek recalls as an exceptional collaboration. Nebenzahl proved to be a very good client, and relations between architect and client were extremely cordial. Koralek still recalls this as an exceptional project. ABK was commissioned to design all the furniture for the house, and a team of excellent craftsmen was recruited. Many of the site labourers were Palestinians and the architects, for all their respect for Nebenzahl, found the political climate of Israel uncomfortable – in more recent years, Peter Ahrends has been a vocal critic of Israeli policy towards the Palestinians. Seen in the uniquely vibrant light of Jerusalem, the house is nonetheless a remarkable creation, clearly within an ancient tradition but equally entirely modern.

above: The Nebenzahl House was an example of contextual modern design, its masonry elevations in tune with the Old City of Jerusalem

Burton House, London

Perhaps because of their locations the Collen and Nebenzahl houses are not as well known as they deserve to be. Richard Burton's own house in London, in contrast, has been widely published and, since the Burtons generously open their house to the public as part of London Open House, has been seen by thousands of visitors. Richard and Mireille Burton had spent more than 30 years of married life living in nineteenth-century houses, where they raised three sons and a daughter, before they were able finally to move into the house they had long dreamed of inhabiting. The move from a Victorian house was a dramatic one – Burton recalls that 'more than a quarter of our old house was circulation – stairs and corridors. In our new house, circulation accounts for just 8% of the space'. By 1983, when he began designing the house, Burton, aged 50, had worked on very large housing projects. He had been chairman of the RIBA's low-energy group – the 'three Ls' (long life/low energy/loose fit) were fundamental to his philosophy of architecture. He set out to design a family house which would mature well. There should be space for children and grandchildren but not a superfluity of spare bedrooms. Both he and Mireille wanted ample space in which to work at home.

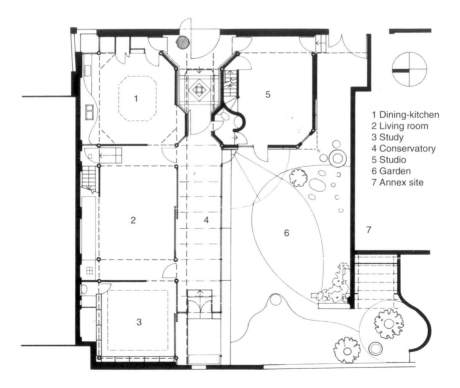

1 Dining-kitchen
2 Living room
3 Study
4 Conservatory
5 Studio
6 Garden
7 Annex site

above: Richard Burton's own house in London's Kentish Town makes good use of a tight site which had never previously been developed

The garden site, land left over from the Victorian development of the area and located just behind their existing house, was sufficiently large to allow for a horizontal, largely single-storey house and for the retention of areas of garden. Burton envisaged that 'we would build it ourselves' – his children had learned the crafts, and two of his sons had trained as furniture makers with John Makepeace at Parnham. This would be a project for the family. All that Burton needed to progress his dream project was time to step back from the practice. When ABK found itself short of work in the aftermath of the National Gallery saga, he decided the time had come and the house went on site in 1986.

The Burton House brought together many influences (including, inevitably, that of ABK's perennial hero, Frank Lloyd Wright) and drew on Richard Burton's background of practice and research over three decades. He had been chairman of the RIBA's low-energy group, and environmental concerns were fundamental to his philosophy of design. North-west London is home to many architects. Among them were many friends of the Burtons – Ted Cullinan, for example, in Camden Mews and Philip Pank in Torriano Cottages. Both the Cullinan and Pank houses, dating from the mid-1960s, made extensive use of timber, and Burton, who was working on the new buildings at Hooke Park in Dorset, was keen to use timber extensively on the house, but perhaps not so prominently as Cullinan and Pank had done. The low-energy agenda was to the fore, and an effect of lightness had to be combined with solidity of construction. The aim was to build a house in which energy consumption was half that of a conventional dwelling of equivalent size, but not one where comfort and delight were entirely sacrificed to the cause of energy saving.

In essence, the Burton House consists of four structural pavilions with a linking conservatory. Three pavilions contain an enfilade of toplit kitchen, living room and study, the second extending to a first floor containing the master bedroom and bathroom. The fourth contains Richard Burton's studio, with an upper storey which can be used as a guest room. The basic structure of the pavilions is a system of posts and beams made of timber, much of it imported from Russia, used in large sections so that it is effectively fireproof. The conservatory, or winter garden, is a steel-and-glass structure (with steel sections detailed in the manner of James Stirling), which provides a layer of insulation between the garden and the living spaces. Partition walls and floors are of brick. The extensive use of timber is the key element in the interior of the house: most of the joinery was the work of Mark and Bim Burton. From the street, the house is almost invisible, screened by a high brick garden wall. It is entered via a circular aluminium gate, which has been described as 'Baggins-like' but which owes its inspiration to the interest of the Burtons' daughter Kate in Chinese art. Most passers-by are unaware that a house lies beyond the gate. The entrance to the house was designed to provide for the retention of a splendid plane tree – a void beneath the house provides space for its roots. From the kitchen, the green expanse of the tree floats above – Burton says

opposite: The interior of the Kentish Town house consists of a series of inter-connected, mostly single-storey spaces

that the tree is the only element in the house needing regular maintenance. The house was completed in three phases in 1987–90. A decade later, Burton added a courtyard house and studio for his daughter on land immediately to the south. Writing in the *Architectural Review*, Peter Davey welcomed the house as an antidote to the prevailing postmodernist fashion: 'it is extraordinary to find a decent new house today because clients are for the most part concerned to demonstrate their vulgarity by buying Pomo rubbish. It is even more strange to find a house of such ingenuity, richness and ecological consciousness in a secret garden behind a wall in Kentish Town'.[5]

Burton, the first of the founding partners of ABK to retire from the practice, has maintained an interest in low-cost, energy-efficient housing. With his friend and neighbour, Eric Reynolds of Urban Space Management, he worked on a scheme for key-worker housing on a small site in Camden Town, using recycled freight containers stacked to provide eight housing units at a modest cost of £700 per square metre (£65 per square foot). The scheme would have housed workers from nearby hospitals, and was seen as a model for the effective use of small sites across inner London, but it was vetoed by Camden Council.[6] Architecture, Richard Burton has written, 'is an holistic activity and, in my opinion, this is the underlying principle that has informed our design intentions. This broad based approach has been lacking in most of the

above: The Burton house is entered via a circular gate from the street – a mature tree was incorporated into the designs

building in the latter half of this century. Over the last two decades we have consciously been involved in filling gaps and extending our expertise in order to produce a more complete architecture'.[7] ABK's housing projects look forward to 'a more complete architecture', in which the theories of functionalism are reconsidered and the needs of real people become the proper focus.

Notes

1   Alan Powers, *Britain: modern architectures in history*, London, Reaktion Books, 2007, pp.70–2.
2   'Building study: Chalvedon housing area, Basildon', *Architects' Journal*, 14 September 1977, pp.491–2.
3   ibid., p.494.
4   ibid., p.500.
5   Peter Davey, 'Tailor made Burton', *Architectural Review*, September 1990, p.43.
6   Paul Finch, 'A small site, but a big idea', *Architects' Journal*, 23 October 2003, pp.22–3.
7   Richard Burton, 'Architecture – towards an holistic approach' in *Ahrends Burton and Koralek*, London, Academy Editions, 1991, p.22.

above: **A conservatory provides a layer of insulation between the living spaces in the Burton house and the enclosed garden**

4   Designing for Commerce

Studying at the AA in the 1950s, Peter Ahrends, Richard Burton and Paul Koralek were immersed in a school where (in Peter Ahrends' words) 'there was a sense of optimism and purpose ... the mood was one of commitment to social change'. After graduating, Burton went to work for the LCC for a time, in what was then the largest architectural office in Europe. Both he and Koralek were employed by Powell & Moya, a practice launched on the strength of the commission for Churchill Gardens, a massive public-housing project. Powell & Moya, in common with the other critically regarded practices of the immediate post-war period, worked almost exclusively for the public sector – schools, universities, hospitals and housing constituted the greater part of their workload. By the 1970s, however, even the most socially committed architects had increasingly to adjust to a changing political and economic climate – the 1980s, with the public sector shrinking in the face of Thatcherite policies, was even more challenging. For Peter Blundell Jones, ABK was 'a pragmatic firm who attempt to make the best of whatever circumstances they find themselves in'.[1] ABK's work for the private sector was driven nonetheless by values that underpinned all the practice's work, in particular by a social programme which prioritised the needs of the users of a building.

Habitat Store and Warehouse, Berkshire

The commission for a new showroom/retail store and warehouse for Habitat on the outskirts of Wallingford, Berkshire (where the company already had a warehouse and offices), came in 1971. Habitat, founded by Terence Conran in 1964, has been credited with transforming public taste in Britain and popularising modern design with its affordable furniture and household goods. Conran (b.1931) had been a contemporary of Richard Burton at Bryanston, and approached Burton when the idea of the Wallingford development emerged – 'he liked our offices', Burton recalls. 'He turned out to be a model client, coming to us with a very clear brief for the scheme.' Conran later recalled: 'I was determined that we should build something that reflected the style of Habitat.'[2] Overcoming the objections of others in the company who favoured an off-the-peg shed, Conran agreed a budget just 20 per cent above that of the latter. Richard Burton ran the project, with Peter Wadley as job architect. Construction began in October 1972, and the buildings were completed early in 1974. The architecture of the scheme, perceived as reflecting Habitat's public image, reflected the blossoming of 'High Tech', with

opposite: The Wallingford development for Habitat included a distribution warehouse as well as a retail store and reflected the company's commitment to good design

industrial production techniques applied to the design of highly flexible buildings. A
precedent was provided by the Reliance Controls factory at Swindon, designed by Team
4 and completed in 1966.

At Wallingford, the huge interior of the warehouse was covered by four steel space-
frame units, each spanning 36 metres by 30 metres (118 by 98 feet) and supported
centrally on a cluster of four concrete columns at the middle of the building – a structural strategy devised by Richard Harryott of Arup. An upper level, containing offices,
extended over half the internal space. The showroom, barely more than 10 per cent
of the size of the warehouse, featured a single space frame. Both buildings, compared

above: Habitat's store at Wallingford, housed in a low-cost supershed, offered a new experience for
shoppers, with a café and children's playground among its amenities

by the architects to a parent and child, were clad with corrugated panels formed
of pre-painted asbestos cement – the warehouse a modish acid green (the colour
of Conran's Porsche), the showroom white, with Habitat's name spelt out in super-
graphics. 'Ample car-parking' was provided – in the early 1970s, space for 50 cars was
thought sufficient. The showroom (which closed in 1995) had a café, with access to an
external terrace – interiors were designed by Conran's own team. A playground for
children was equipped with sculptural equipment by Eduardo Paolozzi. Critic Lance
Wright detected an air of 'desperation' in the project – conventional architectural strategies, he argued, were irrelevant when what the client demanded was 'an ever larger
cubage of blank space which must be provided quicker and quicker and at less cost'.[3] But
the evolution of the out-of-town retail centre from the 1980s on, generating shopping
megastructures, made the Wallingford development seem endearingly human in scale.
And the cheap and cheerful – but intensely stylish – aesthetic of ABK's buildings
seemed entirely in tune with the Habitat philosophy, which infused retailing with an
element of the idealistic.

Cummins Engines Factory, Lanarkshire

The project for a new production plant for the Cummins Engine Company at Shotts
in Lanarkshire, halfway between Glasgow and Edinburgh, began when the American
architect Kevin Roche called ABK's London office in 1975 and spoke to Peter Ahrends.
He said he had recommended ABK to advise Cummins on a new office project, but
the eventual outcome of this conversation was the commission for the new plant at
Shotts. Roche had designed production buildings for Cummins at Darlington in the
north-east of England and in Columbus, Indiana, where he was commissioned to design
the company's corporate headquarters. Cummins had been founded in Columbus in
1919, and under the chairmanship of J. Irwin Miller (1909–2004) it became a global
operation and a world leader in the manufacture of diesel engines – the Shotts factory,
opened in 1956, was its first production facility outside the USA. Miller, whose own
house in Columbus was designed by Eero Saarinen, was a keen patron of architecture
and took a close interest in the plans to expand the Shotts factory complex. The existing
buildings, developed by the Scottish Development Agency in the late 1940s, were little
more than utilitarian – a low-rise factory fronted by an office block. Miller had vetoed
the first plans for extending the facility (more than doubling its production capacity
and workforce) and wanted a building of quality – hence the approach to ABK. Peter
Ahrends proposed a comprehensive redevelopment, in which all production would
take place in the new factory, with the existing buildings converted to offices and
warehousing. Following a meeting with Cummins management on site at Shotts,
Ahrends flew to America to meet Miller and other company executives. The project
was to evolve as a classic example of Ahrends' perennial desire to 'explore the brief,
develop it with a client and seize the opportunities it provided'. For Cummins, Ahrends,
working with Paul Drake (a partner at ABK since 1974), proposed an approach which

above: The site for the Cummins engine factory was in the industrial zone between Edinburgh and Glasgow

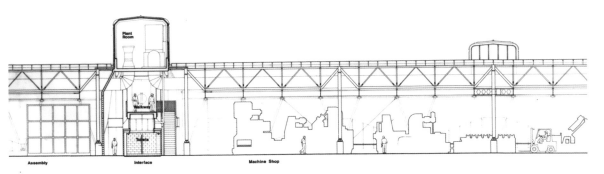

Assembly   Interface   Machine Shop

CUMMINS ENGINE CO. LTD.

Section BB

Scale

top: Section through the Cummins factory at Shotts, Lanarkshire
above: Interior with engines

might have deterred a cautious client: he wished to involve the staff who would work in the new building in the design process. Miller was supportive of this strategy – he was by nature an innovator and interested in new ways of working, and, as an American, free of the rigid conservatism which was a perennial blight on British industry.

The Cummins project was one in which architecture, engineering (structural and services, both by Arup) and social purpose coalesced. The process of consultation involved interviewing around one in five of Cummins' employees at Shotts. Peter Ellis, a sociologist from the LSE who had been recruited to carry out research in connection with ABK's housing projects, organised the interviews and collated the findings. A number of issues came to the fore – those questioned wanted a quieter, airier, more spacious working environment, with views out, and improved canteen and medical facilities. When the factory had first opened in the 1950s, the great majority of the employees came to work by bus; now many arrived in their own cars, and convenient parking was another priority. As the project developed, the demands for better staff amenities had to be considered in the context of the rationale of production. In terms of the planning of the building, the sloping site made it possible to locate parking alongside the factory, with convenient direct access to it via three covered bridges extending north/south at an upper level. Access was provided from two bridges to a deck containing the medical centre and cafeteria, a social hub with views of the production line flowing below on an east/west axis. The structure of the building was planned on a 15-metre (50-foot) grid and formed of tubular steel columns and trusses, with a reinforced-concrete frame supporting the first-floor walkways and the plant rooms at roof level. A double-skin cladding, well insulated, was formed of corrugated steel for the inner skin, with an outer skin of corrugated aluminium sheeting. One of the special features of the factory, completed in 1983, was the provision of natural light and views out from the production level to the surrounding landscape. Undulating window bays were places where workers could take a break and maybe eat a sandwich lunch. Employing up to 2,000 people, Cummins was a major component in the local economy – so the eventual decision to shut the plant and transfer its operations south of the border was a serious blow to the area. It finally closed in 1998. Fortunately, ABK's building had already been listed at Grade A (the equivalent of Grade I in England) and it was subsequently adapted to house a number of small businesses.

Projects for Sainsbury's and W. H. Smith

The early 1980s saw ABK thriving, with up to 50 staff in the office – as large a complement as the practice supported at any time in its half-century of existence. (In the mid-1960s, there had been three architectural assistants and two secretaries.) The workload balanced public and commercial projects. One large company which seemed determined to improve its architectural image was the supermarket giant J. Sainsbury. When the firm began planning a new outlet in the historic city of Canterbury, it decided to hold a limited competition with Norman Foster as architectural assessor. (Foster had

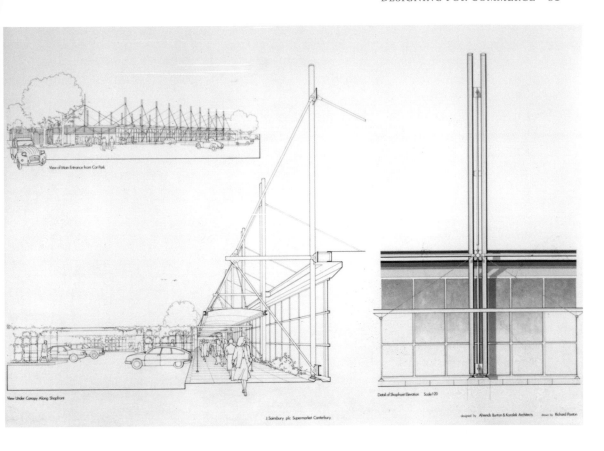

View of Main Entrance from Car Park

View Under Canopy Along Shopfront

Detail of Shopfront Elevation   Scale 1:20

J Sainsbury plc Supermarket Canterbury

designed by Ahrends Burton & Koralek Architects   drawn by Richard Paxton

completed the Sainsbury Centre in Norwich in 1978, a benefaction to the University of East Anglia by the former chairman of the family firm, Robert Sainsbury, and his wife Lisa.) ABK was appointed to design the new store in 1982. The site was east of the city centre, with views across the centre to the cathedral. While describing the resulting building as 'an elegant box', Paul Koralek points out that there are 'references to Gothic' elements in the structure, designed in collaboration with engineer Tony Hunt (who had worked with Foster at Norwich). The metal-deck flat roofs extending over three linked clear-span spaces were suspended from tubular steel masts, which gave the 4,000 square metre (43,000 square foot) building its distinctive appearance. The idea, not new in ABK's work, was to create the impression of a roof floating over unobstructed internal space. Externally, the store, completed in 1984 with the late Richard Paxton as project architect, fronted on to a large car park, its entrance façade clad in a mix of glass and aluminium panels. A fabric canopy, extending along the frontage and suspended from the masts, provided shelter for shoppers. Koralek's only regret about the project

above: Drawings showing details of the elevational treatment of ABK's Sainsbury supermarket in Canterbury

was that the architects had no input to the design of the store's interior, which was a standard Sainsbury fit-out.

Another high-profile commercial client was the retail group W. H. Smith Ltd, which had its headquarters in Swindon. In 1982, ABK was appointed to design a substantial extension to the firm's offices there – Peter Ahrends ran the project, which reflected his interest in low-energy design. The building was naturally ventilated. The plan, a two-storey matrix around landscaped courtyards, allowed offices to benefit from natural light while external automatic blinds baffled solar gain. The aesthetic of the building balanced solid and lightweight elements in a way that had already become one of ABK's trademarks, with a bastion-like reception drum, clad in solid masonry, providing a connection to a diagonal route cutting across the grid – Jeremy Melvin commented that 'the grid represents a continuous ground, the distorting diagonal the notion of individuality and particularity'.[4]

above: Sainsbury's Canterbury store
opposite upper: Plan of WH Smith: the low-energy headquarters featured a diagonal route extending across a grid of office spaces
opposite: Blinds and sun-shading on the elevation of WH Smith

1   Entrance
2   Reception
3   Access route
4   Offices
5   Lift and stairs
6   Car park

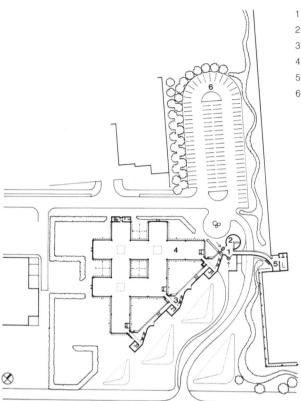

John Lewis Store, Kingston

The John Lewis store at Kingston-upon-Thames, on the western edge of London, remains one of ABK's largest built projects. John Lewis was, in many respects, an ideal client, with its philosophy of partnership and profit-sharing. Its flagship store, Peter Jones in Chelsea, was regarded as one of the best Modern Movement buildings in Britain. Kingston, though now engulfed by the capital's suburbs, is an ancient market town with a fine setting by the River Thames. The site for the new department store was close to Kingston Bridge, an area of semi-derelict land with the potential to provide a link between the town centre, with the existing Bentall's store, and the neglected riverside. John Lewis had expressed an interest in the site as early as 1970, but was initially deterred by the severe traffic congestion which threatened to throttle the centre of Kingston. The commission to ABK came in 1979, though construction began only in 1986, with the store opening in 1990. The delay was due in no small part to the local authority's aim to combine redevelopment of the riverside site with the construction of a major new road link, seen as the solution to the congestion problem, which would

above: The John Lewis store is located alongside the Thames next to Kingston Bridge

traverse it and allow for pedestrianisation of much of the town centre. For a time the road scheme threatened to scupper the John Lewis project, and a way had to be found of making the two work together. Paul Koralek, who led the ABK team with Patrick Stubbings, suggested that the planners might consider a realignment of the route for the road – a further complication was provided by the fact that highway powers were held by the Greater London Council, until the latter was abolished in 1986 and those powers passed to the borough. Instead of snaking through the site, as originally planned, the new road was redesigned as a straight cut diagonally across it. The store was to straddle the road, which occupied what was, in effect, a tunnel cut through the building, dividing it into two unequal triangles. From second-storey level upwards, the floors of the store span across the road.

The process of construction, following the long delays in planning, was complex and protracted. Providing the requisite servicing areas and two floors of parking meant excavating a huge hole to contain three levels of basements – the proximity of the site to the Thames, with the consequent possibility of flooding, necessitated the

above: **The well-mannered street frontage of the John Lewis store responds to the urban context**

construction of a new river wall with a concrete diaphragm wall, up to 18 metres (60 feet) deep, around the perimeter. The engineering of the new relief road was also a key issue: traffic vibration had to be excluded from the store. A further complication was provided by the discovery on site of a stone-vaulted medieval basement, long lost under later development. This structure was carefully removed from site, and later reinstated as a feature of the riverside promenade.

Despite its size – 60,000 square metres (646,000 square feet) of space, including basement car parking – the store has a benign impact at street level: on Wood Street it addressed the bulk of Bentall's store (which has since been redeveloped behind retained façades as a shopping centre), but on Clarence Street to the south the context was one of small-scale buildings, diverse in style and materials, with the ancient parish church of All Saints and the historic marketplace close at hand. A sand-coloured brick was selected as the principal component for the façades of the store, producing an exterior that is far more solid in appearance than the architects initially intended. A rotunda forms a landmark at the junction of Wood Street and Clarence Street – it is the principal point of entry to the store, and houses a coffee shop at first-floor level. One of

above: **Escalators connect the stepped floors in the John Lewis store – the interior is naturally lit**

the local authority's objectives in approving the development of the John Lewis site was
to create an attractive public route along the riverside. ABK's response to the river was
to break down the bulk of the building visually into a number of elements– notably a
prominent tower containing lifts and stairs, with a covered arcade elevated above the
new public walkway. In contrast to many other retail developments of the period – and
others completed since – John Lewis, Kingston, has a strongly civic character, generously embracing, rather than turning its back on, its context. It is clearly a 'contextual'
design, but it pulls no punches in its uncompromising modernity. (Alan Powers has
suggested that the roots of ABK's 'contextual modernism' can be found in pre-war
British Modernism – for example, in the work of Maxwell Fry in the late 1930s.[5])

Successful, however, as the store is as a piece of civic design, its most significant
feature is its stepped, naturally lit interior. It is no exaggeration, indeed, to suggest that
the project represented a bold restatement of the potential of the department store as a
modern building type. The last British department store of real architectural distinction
was Peter Jones, designed in the 1930s but completed, with some compromises, after the
Second World War. But Britain had nothing to match the spectacular stores of Paris
(for example, Printemps and La Samaritaine), with their lofty, galleried, daylit interiors,
which were clearly one source of inspiration to ABK. The invention of the passenger
lift had made these buildings practical. The Kingston store makes virtuoso use of a

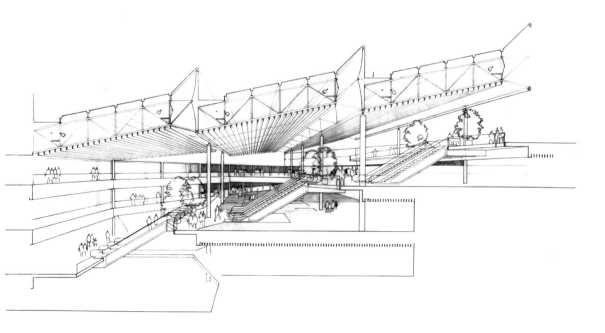

above: Section through the John Lewis store at Kingston upon Thames showing the stepped section

subsequent invention: the escalator. The retail floors are laid out as a series of three stepped terraces arranged on a diagonal axis – generated, of course, by the route of the relief road – and accessed by escalators. The 'diagram' recalls that of Foster Associates' Willis Faber & Dumas office building in Ipswich (completed in 1975) but was equally prefigured by ABK's Portsmouth library, opened in 1977. At Ipswich, the walls are of glass, the roof solid. At Kingston, as on a smaller scale at Portsmouth, the stepped interior is capped, in the tradition of the great nineteenth-century department stores, by a glazed roof, 3,500 square metres (37,600 square feet) of it, channelling daylight into the selling floors (and right down into the Waitrose supermarket which occupies the first basement level). The design of the double-glazed roof incorporates louvres and blinds to counter solar gain, as well as a sprinkler system and provisions for smoke extraction.

Paul Koralek envisaged the interior of the store as a great glazed courtyard, a modern version of the Victorian winter garden. Its subtly daylit space remains unique among British retail buildings, though Koralek points out that, in line with normal practice, John Lewis makes free use of artificial lighting to highlight merchandise – areas beneath the terraces need additional illumination. ABK brought in Vienna-based lighting designer Friedrich Wagner to advise on the lighting strategy for the building. Commercially, the Kingston store was a huge success – it remains John Lewis's biggest selling outlet after the Oxford Street store. There can be little doubt that the concept of a naturally lit space serviced by escalators influenced the subsequent major refurbishments of the latter and of the Peter Jones building, in both cases boosting the commercial performance of the stores.

British Telecom Headquarters, Milton Keynes

ABK's work for commercial clients consistently sought to challenge conventional ideas about the workplace and to focus on the needs of the users of buildings. This was certainly the case with the unbuilt project for a new headquarters for British Telecom in Milton Keynes, the subject of an invited competition in 1983. The brief was for a large building accommodating around 1,500 staff and providing conference, laboratory and archive facilities. ABK broke down the office accommodation into four three-storey pavilions linked by a glazed arcade, with a fifth pavilion housing the reception area and other central facilities. Internally, the office pavilions featured a stepped section, a feature seen in the Portsmouth library and John Lewis store, beneath a glazed roof – the aim was to create a low-energy office environment with savings of up to 40 per cent on energy costs in comparison with conventional air-conditioned buildings. Many of the offices had open views across parkland to the south of the complex, while the parking area to the north was screened by planted trellises. Large trellises supported on the suspension structure of the pavilion roofs carried further planting, the aim being to integrate buildings and landscape.

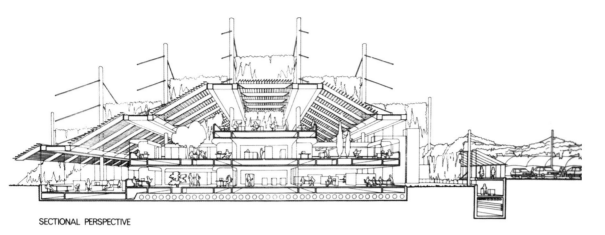

SECTIONAL PERSPECTIVE

Established as one of the most critically rated British architectural practices and with an impressive portfolio of built work, ABK appeared set to benefit from the development boom of the 1980s, when developers were taking an increasingly enlightened approach to the commissioning process. The saga of the National Gallery (where the brief included a substantial speculative office development) was to cause considerable damage to the practice (see pp.97–101), but ABK continued to figure on shortlists for major commercial projects. It was briefly involved in the saga of Paternoster Square, but was not among the practices eventually invited to develop proposals for this site close to St Paul's Cathedral.

Two London Office Schemes

Two major projects for prominent central London sites, both regrettably unrealised, confirmed, that ABK was a contender for big office schemes. The first of these was for a site at the northern end of Shaftesbury Avenue, on the edge of Covent Garden. ABK's first proposal was for a radical refurbishment of the existing (1960s) buildings there, but a scheme for total redevelopment subsequently emerged. Peter Ahrends, who ran the project, draws comparisons with the 'inside/outside' additions to Keble College, Oxford. At Shaftesbury Avenue, the solid elevation presented to the street contrasted with the open, lightweight treatment of the rear façade of the building, with a glazed roof sweeping down in deference to the small-scale properties to the west of the site. The strongly modelled, almost sculptural character of the designs reflected Ahrends' input.

At Stag Place, close to Victoria Station, a high-profile competition was launched by developer Land Securities in 1986 for a new 23,000 square metre (250,000 square foot) office building to replace Eland House on Bressenden Place, part of a 1960s' redevel-

above: **Section of unbuilt BT project in Milton Keynes**

opment of the former Stag brewery site. Among the practices submitting schemes alongside ABK were Richard Rogers Partnership; Arup Associates; Terry Farrell Partnership; Skidmore, Owings & Merrill; and Richard Horden – the last-named the eventual winner. The various submissions (illustrated in the *Architectural Review* of January 1988) offer an intriguing insight into the British architectural scene at the time. The prevailing influence was that of High Tech, but ABK's proposals offered an interesting alternative. In contrast to the formal, orthogonal approach of most of the other submissions, ABK proposed a building strongly organic in character, with two wings of offices, one following closely the line of Bressenden Place. The inner faces of these wings were to be cut back, with glazed upper storeys in the manner of the Shaftesbury Avenue project, and the intervening space would accommodate a covered court, potentially housing a restaurant, health club and other facilities. The street elevation would have a more solid appearance. The aim, the architects declared, was 'to provide Victoria

above: Model of ABK's unbuilt Shaftesbury Avenue project, the curved building towards the top

with a building of strong presence that makes a contribution both at a formal and social level'.[6] Perhaps the scheme was too radical – it did not make the final shortlist of three. This was doubtless a further blow to the partnership. In 1987, Peter Ahrends accepted a chair of architecture at the Bartlett School in London – for the next few years he was to spend 50 per cent of his time as an academic. Richard Burton also took time away from the office to work on his new house in Kentish Town. Paul Koralek was kept busy with the completion of John Lewis at Kingston, but the prospects for future commissions on this scale were uncertain. Staff were laid off as the practice coped with the aftermath of the National Gallery debacle.

Notes

1 Peter Blundell Jones, introduction to *Ahrends Burton and Koralek*, London, Academy Editions, 1991, p.11.

2 Terence Conran, quoted in Kenneth Powell (ed.), *Collaborations: the architecture of ABK*, London, August/Birkhäuser, 2002, p.40.

3 Lance Wright, 'Showroom and warehouse, Wallingford, Berkshire', *Architectural Review,* August 1974, p.79.

4 Jeremy Melvin, 'Maximum revolutions per minute', *Building Design*, 2 June 1995, p.14.

5 Alan Powers, *Britain: modern architectures in history*, London, Reaktion Books, 2007, p.92.

6 *Architectural Review*, January 1988, p.57.

5   The Civic Realm

Over the last half century, ABK has been a partnership in the fullest sense of the word. Peter Ahrends, Richard Burton and Paul Koralek's partnership, launched in 1961, was founded on personal friendship and mutual professional respect. That spirit persisted as additional directors were brought in: Paul Drake, John Hermsen and Patrick Stubbings in 1974, and subsequently Christine Price, Hugh Morgan and David Cruse. But the founders of the practice remained central to its work. Alongside genuine collaboration, there was always an understanding that each partner managed his own projects, once there had been agreement on the direction of the designs – Keble College and the National Gallery, for example, were Ahrends', Richard Burton ran Templeton College and the Moscow Embassy, Paul Koralek the various Dublin projects and John Lewis, Kingston. On every project there was critical input from all the partners. Richard Burton explained the process of collaboration in a lecture of 1971:

> the debate within the group can be time consuming, to be sure, but it is usually successful and, in most instances, a position is reached where we are all agreed. We never vote in order to reach a decision, but occasionally a partner who disagrees will produce an alternative, or we may change the physical location of the group. Once an idea is accepted, it becomes part of group property. As such, each partner's relationship with it keeps it alive, and the idea has a chance of really coming to fruition.[1]

One thing was always clear: each of the partners was involved in the design process as well as in the management of the practice.

Canberra Bell Tower

One project which involved all the partners was a submission for the Canberra Bell Tower competition of 1968. The carillon tower, housing a set of bells, was to be a gift from the British Government to mark the fiftieth anniversary of Australia's federal capital. The site was on an island in one of the city's many parks. Paul Koralek took on the task of visiting the site and developing a collaboration with engineers at Arup (who were working on the Sydney Opera House). ABK's scheme was not selected but it was by far the most memorable of the six submitted, a striking lattice-shell structure taking

opposite: Model of ABK's unsuccessful submission for a proposed bell tower in the Australian capital, Canberra

the form of two great sails framing the central carillon. It was 'an attempt to find a 20th century meaning for the idea of a "monument"', says Koralek. It was certainly an early example of ABK's quest for a new 'language' for public buildings.

St Anne's Church, Soho

Hardly less striking were the designs for St Anne's Church in Soho (1964), on which Richard Burton was the lead partner. The church had been totally destroyed save for S. P. Cockerell's eccentric tower by wartime bombs, leaving the parish to worship in a church hall, but the vicar, Fr John Hester, had a vision of a strikingly modern new church as a spiritual resource for the area. Burton recalls Hester as a remarkable character, much loved by the local community – a progressive thinker, he was tolerant of its remarkable variety; a committed Anglo-Catholic who was a friend to everyone, including prostitutes and the nascent gay community. Fr Hester was enthused by the spirit of liturgical renewal flowing from the Second Vatican Council and wanted a church in which the focus was the central altar. Burton proposed a building which would be a spiritual beacon by day and night, an octagonal space defined by four concrete perimeter columns supporting a lightweight cladding, extending over the roof and walls of the building, formed of metal mesh sandwiched between two layers of glazing. (The structure of the building reflected the need to create a clear space at

above: **Model of the proposed new church of St Anne, Soho**

basement level, which would house parking – this was to be leased to a developer, providing income for the parish.) By day, the church would have a translucent appearance, but by night it would glow. The possibility of commissioning some panels of stained glass from the artist John Piper was discussed. The new St Anne's would have unquestionably have been one of the most remarkable British churches of the post-war era, but the funding package on which the project depended collapsed. The new church remained unbuilt after John Hester moved on, firstly to St Paul's, Covent Garden, then to become vicar of Brighton and subsequently a residentiary canon of Chichester Cathedral (in which role he helped secure a new use for the city's theological college buildings – an early ABK project – after the college's closure).

Post Office Headquarters, London

Another outstanding project which remained sadly unrealised was that for a new headquarters for the Post Office (then a government department) in the City of London. Eric Bedford (1909–2001), Chief Architect at the then Ministry of Public Building and Works from 1951 to 1970, was something of an enthusiast for ABK's work – he had suggested that the practice be shortlisted for the British Library project, won by Leslie Martin and Colin St John Wilson. At Bedford's suggestion, ABK was brought in to rethink the Post Office's development plans. Since the early nineteenth century, the Post Office's central administration had been based at St Martin's le-Grand, just north of St Paul's. It occupied several large blocks of Edwardian date, one of them backing on to the green space of Postman's Park. The Post Office's plans for a new headquarters, under consideration since the mid-1960s, coincided with plans by the City of London to reconfigure the road network in the area – disgracefully, half of the surviving shell of Christopher Wren's war-damaged Christ Church, Newgate, was demolished for road widening and the plan was also to demolish the block overlooking Postman's Park. A new building on the site would conform to the new road line. Fortunately, attitudes were changing and the new building was relocated at the suggestion of ABK to occupy the empty site of the former Telegraph Office, which had been destroyed by bombing in 1940.

ABK's scheme was little short of revolutionary in the context of office design in Britain in the early 1970s. The concept of open-plan office space – *Bürolandschaft* – was regarded with some suspicion by developers, clients and users. In proposing mostly open-plan offices for the Post Office, ABK faced potential opposition but a process of consultation, involving the trade unions and with senior managers and union nominees visiting recent office developments in Germany and Sweden, helped convince the doubters. The plan of the new building, which would entirely fill the island site, consisted of two segments of floor space separated by a service core. At the south-west and north-east corners of the block landscaped piazzas were connected to pedes- trian bridges spanning the adjacent streets – a planning requirement and part of the City's continuing preoccupation with segregating pedestrians and traffic but allowing

above: Model of the unbuilt scheme for a new Post Office headquarters in the City of London

the public to walk through the building. The latter was to be fully glazed but with a layer of metal latticework superimposed on the façades, incorporating sun screening and window-cleaning gear but equally an aesthetic device. The *Architectural Review* commented: 'in other words, this filigree is the ornament of the Modern Movement, which in its own way sets out to fulfil some of the function of the ornament of tradition … The PO should prove to be the most "sociable" and therefore the most acceptable big intruder on the City streets since the war.'[2] In 1975, however, with Britain in economic crisis and savage cuts being made in public spending, the project was cancelled, even as the ABK office was completing the working drawings. The cancellation of the project was a huge blow to the practice. A dismal building designed by the Property Services Agency's in-house architects later filled the site.

National Gallery Extension

ABK was never able to make its mark on the streets of central London, but for a brief time it appeared that an ABK building would occupy as prominent a site as the capital could offer. The practice's success in the competition for an extension to the National Gallery – and the subsequent abandonment of its scheme in the context of bitter public debate – was a watershed in ABK's history. The site of the old Hampton's store, immediately to the west of William Wilkins's National Gallery, had lain empty since its clearance by wartime bombing. It was an obvious site for an extension to the gallery, but the Conservative Government elected in 1979 was unwilling to provide public funding for the project. Instead, Environment Secretary Michael Heseltine proposed an ingenious, if in the event flawed, solution whereby a developer would build the new galleries (intended to house the Early Renaissance collections) in return for being allowed to construct lettable offices as part of the development. So an open architect/developer competition was launched in December 1981. ABK was invited to work with Trafalgar House, and in April 1982 its scheme was one of 80 submitted. The submissions were judged by a panel which included Lord Annan, Chairman of the Gallery's trustees; its Director, Michael Levey; and Sir Hugh Casson, one of Britain's best-known architects, then President of the Royal Academy and an enthusiast for ABK's work, as well as several professional advisors.

Seven schemes were shortlisted – those by ABK; Arup Associates; Covell Matthews & Wheatley; Richard Rogers; Sheppard Robson; Raymond Spratley Partnership; and Skidmore, Owings & Merrill (SOM), the latter a major American practice in the process of establishing a presence in London. Colin Amery, writing in the *Financial Times*, commented that ABK

> *have understood the need for intellectual formality in this building. They*
> *have designed a bold horseshoe-shaped building with a curved facade round*
> *a court and side elevations that respect the streets. Their particular success*
> *has been the barrel-vaulted galleries, the walls slightly curving (difficult to*
> *hang large pictures!) that are spaces resonant with an understanding of the*

> need for the building to respond to the lasting qualities of the Renaissance
> pictures. It is also a strongly balanced response to the stone classicism of the
> Square.³

In late summer 1982, the developed schemes of the seven shortlisted practices
were put on public exhibition in the gallery and the public invited to vote for their
favourite. ABK's scheme got the most votes, and in October ABK was named as one of
three finalists with Arup Associates and SOM. Richard Rogers' exuberantly High Tech
scheme (described by Colin Amery as 'manic' and 'coarse'), featuring a prominent tower,
was not shortlisted. Just before Christmas, the partnership of ABK/Trafalgar House
was named as the final winner.

The way appeared clear for the ABK scheme, which placed three floors of offices below
the top-floor gallery level and was both respective to its context and clearly modern, to be
built, but many hurdles lay in its path. In particular, the National Gallery trustees were
not happy with some aspects of the winning scheme – a number of them had wanted
the SOM scheme, a sober (some thought dull) exercise in postmodern Classicism. Henry
Moore, a friend of Richard Burton's mother, caused dismay in the family when he publicly
spoke in favour of SOM. The great curved gallery spaces circling the central court, which
Amery had judged a 'particular success', were strongly criticised by two artist trustees,
Bridget Riley and Howard Hodgkin, while it was pointed out that the SOM scheme would
have provided rather more gallery space than ABK's.

There was a move to put aside the result of the competition and appoint SOM.
Michael Heseltine was, however, forthright when he met the trustees a couple of
weeks before the public announcement of the outcome of the competition. He 'assured
them that if ABK's scheme did not satisfy them the DoE would not impose it on them.
The trustees were free to reject it. But that would be that. They would not get their
extension.'⁴ The trustees had little choice but to work with ABK to refine the winning
scheme. Trafalgar House was unhappy about the delay in proceeding to securing
planning permission and concerned about the extra costs involved. But, with the
developer given some reassurances by the government regarding its costs, ABK duly
began work on a revised design, which was first presented to the trustees in June 1983,
with discussions between the architect and the National Gallery continuing over the
next six months.

The revised scheme was inevitably, in many respects, a compromise. In discussion
with the trustees, the need to considerably increase the total area of galleries was
agreed: the curved gallery spaces vanished in favour of more conventional rectangular
rooms, providing 17 galleries in all. As a result, the central court was much reduced
in scale and was no longer the focus of the scheme. A second major change was the
addition of a glazed tower, topped by a coffee shop (an addition to the original brief),
which would also now house the main point of entry to the new galleries. The tower
was perhaps a response to the Rogers scheme (which had gained a degree of popular
and critical support, including praise from the then President of the RIBA, Owen Luder,
for the 'sod you' attitude it seemed to embody). It was seen as a counterbalance to the

above: Presentation sketches and model shots of ABK's first National Gallery scheme, which included a dramatic curving gallery space

elegant tower of James Gibbs's St Martin-in-the-Fields at the far corner of Trafalgar Square. By December 1983, a year after ABK had been named as architect for the extension, the new designs were ready to be made public. Some of the gallery trustees were still unhappy with the designs, but Lord Annan gave them his backing and they went to Westminster Council for planning permission.

In view of the considerable debate over the project, the decision by the new Environment Secretary, Patrick Jenkin, that the revised scheme should be 'called in' to a public inquiry was not unexpected, and a hearing was duly convened in April 1984. The inspector found in favour of the scheme with some reservations about the detailed design of the tower, suggesting that the masts capping it might be omitted. The Secretary of State, however, concluded that the tower would be 'alien to the character of the existing buildings in the vicinity and would constitute an unwelcome intrusion into the square'. On this pretext, in September 1984, he formally refused planning consent for the extension. The decision was a body blow to the practice, but there had been gloom about the prospects of the scheme since 30 May, when the Prince of Wales had spoken at the RIBA's 150th anniversary dinner held at Hampton Court. In the first of a series of well-publicised interventions into the field of architecture and planning, the Prince had lambasted ABK's proposals: 'instead of designing an extension to the elegant facade of the National Gallery which complements it and continues the concept of columns and domes, it looks as if we may be presented with a kind of vast municipal fire station, complete with the sort of tower that contains the siren'. He continued: 'what is proposed is like a monstrous carbuncle on the face of a much-loved and elegant friend'.[5]

above: **Perspective of ABK's second proposal for the National Gallery extension**

Peter Ahrends met Nigel Broackes of Trafalgar House on the morning after the speech (which was widely reported in the press).'He was convinced that the scheme was dead in the water. We were all very shocked at the nature of the intervention'. It remains unclear to what extent the Hampton Court speech influenced Jenkin's decision, but Ahrends is convinced that it was instrumental in wrecking the National Gallery project. Nor is it clear how far Jenkin, in finally abandoning his predecessor's idea of a gallery extension funded by commercial development, was aware that alternative funding would soon be made available. In 1985, Sir John (later Lord) Sainsbury, a gallery trustee, announced that he and his two brothers, Simon and Timothy, were willing to fund the extension. A number of architects were invited to submit proposals – all in a broadly postmodern classical manner – and that by Venturi Scott Brown was selected for what became the Sainsbury Wing, which opened in 1991.

Some time after the abandonment of the ABK scheme, Peter Ahrends found himself invited to a dinner at Kensington Palace, and seated next to the Prince. An attempt at reconciliation followed. The Prince was invited to visit the ABK office in Chalcot Road, NW1. He came to lunch, a polite occasion but, in Ahrends' words, 'rather odd. He looked at some of our work with apparent approval and said, presumably referring to the National Gallery, "I'm sorry it had to be you." Richard Burton's response was: "not half as sorry as we were!"'. The effect of the Hampton Court speech was to be very damaging for ABK – potential clients feared that any project designed by them might fuel royal disapproval and lead to problems with gaining planning consent.

Mary Rose Museum, Portsmouth

In fact, ABK had come to the notice of Prince Charles a couple of years before the National Gallery competition. The practice had won a competition in 1980 to design a museum to house the remains of the *Mary Rose*, a Tudor warship which had sunk in the Solent, close to Portsmouth, in 1545. Plans to raise the well-preserved wreck had been under discussion since the early 1970s, with the Mary Rose Trust being launched in 1979 with the Prince as its Patron. ABK's winning scheme was developed with Robin Wade as exhibition designer and James Hope responsible for landscape design. The problem was that the site chosen for the new museum was at Eastney, a considerable distance from Portsmouth city centre and the historic dockyard. The architects felt that the dockyard would be a far better location for it, and in due course the Prince took the same view. His opinion of ABK's proposals was unclear, but the practice did not warm to his idea that all work on the project should be done for no fee. In due course the site for the museum was moved to the dockyard, but ABK's scheme, featuring a dramatic 'wave' roof, was not built. (After several changes of architect, a new museum building was due to open there in 2012.)

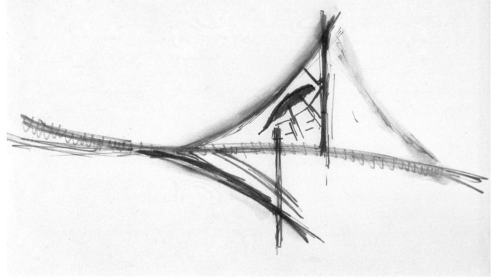

top: Model shot of the proposed Mary Rose Museum
above: Peter Ahrends' sketch for the proposed Mary Rose Museum in Portsmouth

St Mary's Hospital, Isle of Wight

The oil crisis of the early 1970s forced the architectural profession to think seriously about issues of energy conservation. ABK's Felmore housing in Basildon (420 units, begun in 1974) was at the time the largest passive solar scheme anywhere. In 1976, Burton took on the role of coordinator of the RIBA's Energy Initiative, later serving as RIBA Presidential Advisor on energy matters and as a member of several scientific committees examining energy-conservation issues. These were explored in projects such as the Cummins factory and the W. H. Smith offices. But the landmark project in this area was undoubtedly St Mary's Hospital on the Isle of Wight, on which the practice began work in 1981, building on research undertaken over the previous two years in association with the Building Design Partnership (BDP) and engineers Gifford & Partners. It was ABK's first hospital, and the commission was a bold move on the part of the National Health Service (NHS). In terms of its planning, the 191-bed hospital followed the Nucleus template taken up by the NHS in the mid-1970s. It was to become 'a brilliant demonstration of how the component elements of the Nucleus system could be deployed to create an efficient hospital with a unique identity that was both exciting and welcoming to patients and staff'.[6] At St Mary's, ABK eschewed the standard orthogonal Nucleus plan in favour of one in which ward and clinical blocks radiate from a curved circulation 'street', providing a link to the existing hospital buildings, with landscaped garden courts between the blocks. The plan was one element in a design strategy aimed at producing a building using 50 per cent of the energy of a conventional hospital of the same size – along with Wansbeck Hospital in Northumberland, designed by Powell & Moya, St Mary's was intended to be a demonstration model for a new generation of low-energy NHS hospitals.

The configuration of the radiating blocks allowed the wards to benefit from generous natural light, while in clement weather opening windows were the source of venti-lation. The use of aluminium and stainless steel cladding, on a blockwork base and with a high degree of insulation, was a practical as much as an aesthetic device, reflecting heat outwards on warm days and bouncing natural light into the building. A major saving on energy costs was achieved through recycling heat – ABK had established that nearly a quarter of the energy use in a typical Nucleus hospital was generated by the kitchens, which were often uncomfortably warm places in which to work. A sophis-ticated heat-recovery system at St Mary's was accommodated within a walk-through services spine incorporated into the roof and serving top-floor wards to either side. Essentially functional, its curved form was a distinctive feature of the wards, which were airy spaces, naturally top-lit, with no suspended ceilings. Recycled heat was directed to a central energy unit to be stored and reused. The hospital was innovative in other respects: the incorporation of art works and the provision of a landscaped setting were key aspects of the project. Richard Burton commented: 'from the start I took very seriously a study that seemed to confirm what most of us instinctively know: that harmonious surroundings – natural and man made – actually speed the healing process'.[7]

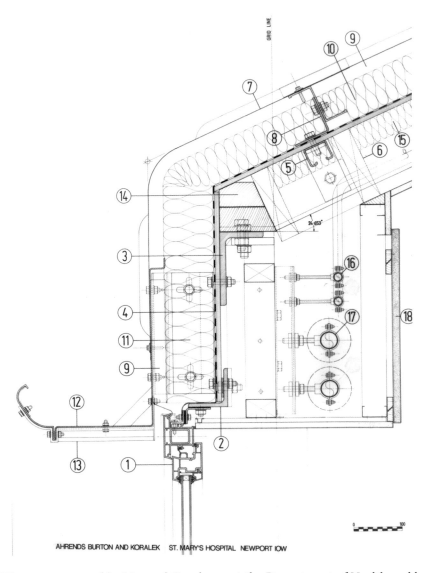

AHRENDS BURTON AND KORALEK   ST. MARY'S HOSPITAL NEWPORT IOW

ABK was encouraged by Howard Goodman at the Department of Health and by the regional health authority, to include art commissions in the scheme, and eventually a full-time arts coordinator was appointed to work at St Mary's. The performing arts – music, dance and theatre – as well as the visual were part of a remarkable arts programme at the hospital in the development, in which Burton took a leading role. The landscape around the hospital, designed by James Hope and including a lake, was seen as a work of art in its own right. There were some teething problems with the hospital – the steel cladding had to be replaced, removing some of the building's sparkle – but it

above: Section through the façade of St Mary's Hospital
opposite: St Mary's Hospital was an exercise in low-energy design, built to a strictly controlled NHS budget

remains a pioneering landmark in hospital design. Whatever its flaws – and critic Colin Davies found its appearance 'disconcerting' rather than reassuring – it is also a work of clear idealism.[8]

The ethos of the Thatcher era, one which the founding partners of ABK found uncongenial, was one of privatisation and the retreat of the state. However, something of a counterbalance was provided by the regeneration policies pursued by Michael Heseltine as Environment Secretary between 1979 and 1983. Although politically contentious, since they took over planning powers from elected local authorities, the London Docklands Development Corporation (established in 1981) and the other development corporations established in a number of provincial cities had some success in regenerating urban areas where traditional industries had declined or vanished. Similar aims drove the series of National Garden Festivals, the first of which took place in Liverpool in 1984 – ABK under Richard Burton, with engineering input from Arup, designed the main pavilion for the 1986 Stoke-on-Trent festival, which took the form of a series of cones clad in PVC-coated fabric.

above: **At St Mary's Hospital landscaping was a key feature**

Docklands

The focus of regeneration in London Docklands was the Isle of Dogs where Canary Wharf emerged as an alternative financial quarter, rivalling the City of London. The first phase of the Docklands Light Railway (DLR), providing a vital public transport link to the Isle of Dogs, opened in 1987, with branches from Tower Gateway, in the City, and Stratford terminating at Island Gardens. The same year saw ABK commissioned to design ten new stations on an 8 kilometre (5 mile) extension of the system from Poplar eastwards through the former Royal Docks to Beckton. The stations were to be simple, economical structures, though the brief was to improve on the design of those on the first section of the DLR system while retaining elements of continuity. Providing effective connections between the stations and their neighbourhood contexts was considered a priority. Some stations were at ground level, others elevated on a viaduct, requiring lift access. Some stations had two platforms, others a single 'island'. ABK's approach – in contrast to that subsequently applied on the stations of the Jubilee Line Extension – was one of 'flexible standardisation', the use of a kit of parts. Peter

above: Sunset at Poplar station of the DLR, including a bridge over a busy highway

ELLX CANOPY 3.2.93

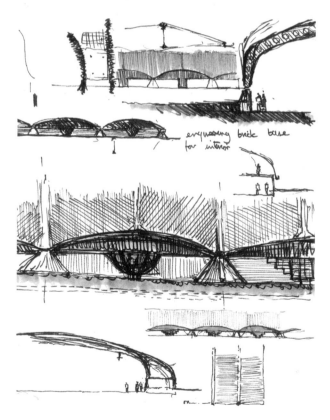

engineering brick base
for interior

top: Section through East London Line station on elevated viaduct
above: Drawing for the North Pole depot

Ahrends commented: 'it is completely standard, but the standard had to be designed to be capable of being varied. In manufacturing terms, the kit was a well understood set of components that were reproducible'.[9] A lightweight cantilevered canopy, highly transparent in form – in contrast to the clumsy steelwork of the original stations – could be adapted to the specific requirements of all the stations on the extension. Lifts, where needed, were painted a bright red and conceived as beacons marking the presence of the DLR. This practical, low-key project generated one structural tour de force: the pedestrian bridge at Poplar, a steel-and-glass tube suspended from a cable-stay structure, which continues the theme of transparency seen in the stations along the line and glows at night as a band of light. There were other, unrealised rail projects, including proposed stations on the East London Line (now part of the London Overground), works to Oxford Circus Underground station and the North Pole depot, near Paddington station, which was to service the Eurostar trains which began operating in 1992.

above: **Techniquest, Cardiff Bay**

Techniquest, Cardiff Bay

Another former dockland area, that of Cardiff, provided a site for Techniquest, billed
as 'a fun palace with a serious mission – to turn children of all ages on to the wonders
of science and technology'. Techniquest had been in existence for over a decade (it
began operations in a converted shop) before it moved into its new home designed by
ABK under Paul Koralek in Cardiff Bay. The funding for the £3.7 million project was
provided by the Cardiff Bay Development Corporation. ABK's Techniquest was not a
new building but an imaginative conversion and extension of an 1890s' ship-repair shed,
unlisted but one of the few structures in the docks surviving from Cardiff's heyday as
the world's largest coal-exporting port. The great iron-framed structure made an ideal
container for a variety of hands-on exhibits – extensions at the north and west end of
the building house a lecture theatre, laboratory, workshops, storage and plant, leaving
the original shed free of clutter as 'a dazzling, cathedral-like hall bathed in daylight,
which floods in through full-height, clear-glazed window walls on the south and east
elevations ... Techniquest's exhibition hall is the antithesis of both the gloomy heritage
shrine and the electronic virtual-reality black box that have become the norm for
museums.' [10] Both Techniquest and the DLR extension reflected ABK's ability to work
with limited means to achieve highly practical results.

British Embassy, Moscow

The Thatcher era was one of strained relations with the Soviet Union – Margaret
Thatcher endorsed Ronald Reagan's description of the USSR as 'the evil empire'. Plans
for constructing a new British Embassy in Moscow were the subject of extended and
sometimes tortuous negotiations. The embassy (both the chancery and the ambassador's residence) had occupied a former aristocratic mansion at Sofiskiiaya Embankment,
looking across the Moscow River to the Kremlin, since 1929. The building was leased
from the Russian Government, which wanted to take it over for use as a museum –
the final renewal of the lease was for just a year. Conveniently, the lease on the Soviet
Embassy in London was also expiring, so a reciprocal agreement acceptable to both
countries was the rational way forward. A site for a new British Embassy had been
identified – at Smolenskaya Embankment, across the river from the existing embassy.
By 1987, agreement was reached between London and Moscow, and plans for the new
British Embassy could proceed. Following a competitive interview process, ABK was
formally appointed that year by the Foreign & Commonwealth Office (FCO) to design
the new building, one of a series of new UK embassies around the world. For Richard
Burton, as partner in charge, the project was significant on several levels: it was to be
the culmination of his career in architecture and also a point of reconnection with his
Russian roots.

   Relations between Britain and the Soviet Union were actually less tense than they
had been a few years earlier, but the Cold War was still a reality and the designs for the

embassy had to provide for a high degree of security. So much so that large elements
of the building were to be shipped ready-made from Britain to avoid the possibility of
electronic 'bugs' being built into the structure. The proposed 'diagram' provided for
residential wings flanking a central pavilion, with offices set back within a glazed court.
The plans were unveiled in the summer of 1991, the critic Hugh Pearman comparing the
impact of the building on the riverside to that of the Festival Hall on the Thames.[11] The
publication of the designs coincided, however, with a change of direction at the FCO.
Mikhail Gorbachev's efforts to reform the USSR failed, and at the end of 1991 the Soviet
Union collapsed: Moscow was now the capital of the Russian Federation and a new era
of international relations had begun. It was decided that the embassy scheme should be
completely rethought. Mark Bertram, Head of the FCO's Overseas Estates Department
(and effectively ABK's client) recalled that the new scheme emerged almost fully
formed – 'it was a pretty clear disposition of functions and it appealed immediately.
Each way that you tested something, the proposal either had an answer or an answer
could readily be fitted into it'.[12] In place of a single monolithic block, the new embassy
scheme was conceived as a series of four separate pavilions linked by high-level bridges

above: The British Embassy occupies a prominent position on the banks of the River Moskva

and capped with timber roofs, three of them containing residential accommodation (31 apartments for staff and their families), the fourth offices and formal spaces.

The new scheme reflected the sea change in relations between Russia and Britain. One consequence of the collapse of communism was that Russian citizens were increasingly free to travel abroad – in the mid-1980s, two British Embassy staff could handle all applications, mainly official, for visas to visit Britain. Today, more than 50 staff are employed, issuing around 14,000 visas a month. The commercial department of the embassy also expanded as trade between Russia and Britain grew and free enterprise replaced universal state ownership. The embassy became a far more open place, and the architecture reflected this transformation. For Richard Burton, 'the Moscow embassy was a pathfinder, just as the Berkeley Library was in Dublin in 1965. They both gave their great cities modern design that was not familiar locally at the time.'[13] However, the new designs were not to the taste of Moscow's Mayor, Yuri Lushkov, who thought they lacked the *gravitas* appropriate to their function and reportedly compared them to a series of blocks of holiday flats on the Black Sea. After 15 months of discussion, in which Burton and Mark Bertram argued the case for the FCO supported by the new ambassador, Sir Andrew Wood the Mayor finally gave his approval after seeing a new

above: **The entrance hall of the Moscow Embassy has an appropriate dignity and generosity of space**

perspective of the proposed building under snow – 'he said it had now become part of Russia', Burton recalls.

The embassy went on site late in 1996 and was opened in 2000. For Burton, 'the embassy took all the skills I had learnt and more' – he paid tribute to the strength of the team working on the project, led by Patrick Stubbings, with John Hermsen and input from Jeremy Peacock. The ABK site team was led by Hugh Morgan, who commuted to Moscow, Robert Davys, and subsequently Barry McCullough based in Moscow.[14] The completed building embodies what Burton sees as key themes in ABK's work: a concern for context, a passionate interest in materials (with the use of timber echoing an old Russian tradition), the provision of generous natural light (in a country where winter brings long hours of darkness), a commitment to low-energy design, and a belief in the incorporation of works of art into buildings. This last was a particular interest of Richard Burton's. Among the artists commissioned to provide works for the embassy – some of them incorporated into the building, others funded by the Government Art Collection – were Tess Jaray, Norman Ackroyd, Michael Craig-Martin, Langlands & Bell, Alex Hartley, Liliane Lijn and Alexander Beleschenko. Furniture was commis-

above: **View from inside one of the offices in the Embassy**

sioned or bought from Fred Scott, Alan Irvine, Ron Arad, Terence Conran and Luke Hughes. The landscape around the building was the work of James Hope, an established ABK collaborator. More than a decade on, the embassy still reflects 'ABK at their most optimistic, bringing promise of the new into the Stygian gloom of a smog-laden Moscow sunset'.[15] Anne Pringle (former British Ambassador) considered the embassy 'the most glorious building I have worked in'.

Art and Opera: Manchester and Compton Verney

ABK's involvement with the visual arts, which dated back to the earliest years of the practice, continued. The practice was commissioned to plan a major extension to Manchester University's Whitworth Art Gallery. The sculpture court there was completed in 1995 (and won an RIBA Award the following year), but the remainder of the scheme remained unexecuted.[16] A competition to design a new opera house in the park at Compton Verney, Northamptonshire, saw ABK on a shortlist of six with a remarkable submission which proposed an auditorium entirely enclosed in glass. The competition was won by Henning Larsen, but the opera house was never built.[17]

above: Interior of Whitworth Art Gallery, Manchester

above: Interior perspective of ABK's competition scheme for the proposed Compton Verney opera house

Civic Commissions in Ireland: Offaly and North Tipperary

Winning the prestigious Moscow commission was a vindication of ABK's high standing among British practices, but by the early years of the twenty-first century its focus was equally on Ireland. After the recession of the 1980s, Ireland began to boom in the next decade and ABK's Irish arm, eventually to become a separate practice, was well placed to profit, completing a number of educational buildings (see Chapter 2) as well as securing commissions for new public buildings. ABK was shortlisted in the 1996 competition for

top: The Offaly County Offices at Tullamore in Ireland
above: The drum of the council chamber is a prominent element of the Nenagh civic offices
opposite: Main concourse, Offaly County Offices

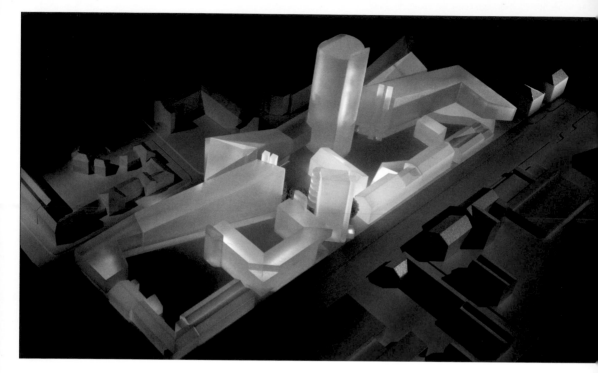

a major extension to the National Gallery of Ireland, but lost out to Benson + Forsyth. However, the practice completed two new civic buildings for local authorities, funded by the flourishing Celtic tiger economy. The offices for Offaly County Council in Tullamore, for which John Parker was director in charge working with Paul Koralek, occupied the site of a former Victorian villa, close to the neo-classical 1830s court house. The skilfully conceived plan allowed a walled garden on the site to be retained, with a new enclosed entrance courtyard to the street. From the courtyard, a linear, tapering atrium extends through the three-storey building and provides an exhibition space and access to a single-storey extension containing a café and crèche overlooking a new enclosed garden. The timber screening enclosing the building incorporates shutters which are part of a natural ventilation strategy. The most formal space, the council chamber, is given a distinctive presence by the use of stone and render cladding. Internally, its sweeping timber roof is, Koralek admits, 'a nod to Aalto'.

The Offaly commission was followed by that for new civic offices for North Tipperary Council in Nenagh. The brief was to create a base not only for the county council but also the town council (given its own council chamber) and local health board. The plan of the building provided for phased development, with office wings extending off a double-height linear concourse. As in Tullamore, the building is prefaced by a new civic space in which the county council's chamber is a dominant

above: Model of the masterplanning concept for the Convent Lands site in Dublin.

element, a drum clad in grey granite. The low-energy agenda pursued at Tullamore was taken further in this project, in which ABK confronted 'the often glib truisms of modern Ireland'.[18] ABK's engagement with master-planning projects in Ireland – for example, for the Convent Lands quarter of Dublin, where a new civic centre was proposed, and an area of the former docklands – reflected the degree to which the practice had become naturalised, as it were, in Ireland. When the Dublin office moved towards independent existence, it did so with the support of the founding partners. The ease with which ABK adapted itself to the society and culture of another country reflects the continuing strength of the principles on which the practice was founded.

Conclusion

The partnership of Peter Ahrends, Richard Burton and Paul Koralek was formally wound up in 2012. Launched in 1961, when the three founding partners were in their late twenties, the practice remained a potent force in British architecture for half a century. Emerging from the Architectural Association at a time when the New Brutalism was the dominant fashion in the school, Ahrends, Burton and Koralek were prepared to swim against the tide. Corbusier was certainly an influence on their work, as on that of others of their generation, but a more pervasive presence was that of Frank Lloyd Wright, whose vision of "the thing growing out of the nature of the thing" was a corrective to the universalism of the Modern Movement. Looking back on a corpus of work that extends over five decades, it is the diversity of ABK's architecture that impresses. There never was a house style, partly because each partner ran his own projects (though each reflected the input of the other two partners) and put his particular stamp on them. For ABK, there were no easy solutions. Each project was the subject of a process of investigation, debate and experiment in which two issues were always to the fore, those of social benefit and impact on context. People and places have an individual identity and it is the task of the architect, ABK always believed, to address that identity, whether the building's user was an Oxford student or a Sainsbury's shopper, and the location Moscow or Basildon. As early as the 1970s, ABK was pioneering in its quest for an environmentally benign modern architecture. Perhaps the most remarkable fact about the partnership was its longevity. Other partners and associates contributed greatly to the success of the practice, but the founders always remained at the heart of the operation, three strong and very different personalities who remain the close friends they had been at the AA back in the 1950s. Some of ABK's most remarkable projects – the Post Office headquarters in the City of London and St Anne's Church, Soho, for example – were never realised. Last year, one of the practice's best buildings, the public library at Redcar, was needlessly destroyed. The legacy of post-war British modernism remains a subject of intense debate but the work of ABK, defying easy categorisation, offers a source of inspiration to new generations of architects for whom the impact of buildings on people, places and the natural environment is an issue which needs to be addressed more urgently than at any time in history.

Notes

1   'Small group design and the idea of quality', *RIBA Journal*, June 1971, p.232.
2   Lance Wright, 'Art object for the Post Office', *Architectural Review*, July 1975, pp.5–6.
3   Colin Amery, 'Seven new schemes for the National Gallery', *Financial Times,* 24 August 1982.
4   Stephen Gardiner and Lawrence Marks, 'Heseltine's Heavy Hand', *Observer Review*, 1 April 1984, p.17.
5   Prince Charles, quoted in Charles Jencks, *The Prince, the Architects and New Wave Monarchy*, London, Academy Editions, 1988, p.43.
6   Sunand Prasad (ed.), *Changing Hospital Architecture*, London, RIBA Publishing, 2008, p.38.
7   Richard Burton, 'St Mary's Hospital, Isle of Wight: a suitable background for caring', *British Medical Journal*, 22–29 December 1990, p.1423.
8   Colin Davies, 'Hospitality', *Architects' Journal*, 3 July 1991, p.31.
9   Peter Ahrends, quoted in Ruth Slavid, 'ABK's kit of parts builds 10 light-rail stations', *Architects' Journal*, 27 April 1994, p.13.
10 Martin Spring, 'Light entertainment', *Building*, 21 July 1995, p.39.
11 Hugh Pearman, *Sunday Times*, 9 June 1991, p.10.
12 Mark Bertram quoted in Kenneth Powell (ed.), *Collaborations: the architecture of ABK*, London, 2002, p.165.
13 'Threads and connections', lecture to the Architectural Association, 26 October 2010.
14 ibid.
15 *Building Design*, 2 June 1995, p.16, Mark Bertram *Room for Diplomacy, Britain's Diplomatic Buildings Overseas 1800–2000,* London, 2011, pp.431–40
16 See Jeremy Melvin, 'Art behind a respectable facade', *Building Design*, 9 July 1993, p.8.
17 See John Welsh, 'Haute culture', *Building Design*, 15 September 1989, p.12.
18 *Architecture Ireland*, October/November 2005, p.59.

List of Works

Substantially altered or partly demolished = *
Demolished = **
Unbuilt projects = ***

1961
Bryan Brown House
Thurlestone, Devon
Client: Mr Bryan Brown

1961
New London Gallery *
Exhibition of Henry Moore and Ben Nicholson
Client: Marlborough Fine Art Ltd

1961–7
Berkeley Library, Trinity College Dublin
Dublin, Republic of Ireland
Client: Trinity College Dublin
Architect & Building News, 14 January 1961
Architects' Journal, 15 June 1961, pp.871–83
Builder, 16 June 1961, pp.1138–46
Architect & Building News, 31 August 1966,
pp.375–8
Architectural Design, October 1967, pp.459–68
Architectural Forum, October 1967, pp.78–85
Architectural Review, October 1967, pp.264–77
Architectural Forum, December 1969, pp.70–5
Architectural Review, December 1969, pp.444–6
Architects' Journal, 26 July 1972, pp.205–16
Architectural Review, July 1979, pp.35–45
RIBA Journal, October 1997, pp.68–75
Christine Casey, *Buildings of Ireland, Dublin*,
Yale University Press, Newhaven & London,
2005, pp.406–7
Building Design, 4 December 2009, pp.18–19

1961–5
**Study and residential accommodation,
Chichester Theological College***
Chichester, West Sussex
Client: Chichester Theological College
Builder, 24 August 1962, p.368
Architect & Building News, 9 January 1963, p.42
Architectural Review, August 1965, pp.90–6
Architect & Building News, 11 August 1965,
pp.263–9
Architects' Journal, 18 August 1965, pp.387–98
Maison, November 1965, pp.360–3
Zodiac, 18, 1968, pp.70–1
Architecture d'Aujourd'hui, December/January
1971–2, pp.64–7

TCD Arts Faculty

1963
Kasmin Gallery**
Bond Street, London
Client: Kasmin Ltd
Architectural Review, November 1963, pp.341–3
Oxford Art Journal, February 2007, pp.233–68

1964
St Anne's Church***
Soho, London
Client: Rector of St Anne's, Soho, and London
Diocesan Fund
Architectural Review, January 1966, p.75
Architecture d'Aujourd'hui, December/January
1971–2, pp.81–3

1965–72
Roman Catholic Chaplaincy
Old Palace, St Aldgate's, Oxford
Client: Trustees of the Newman Trust
Architects' Journal, 10 November 1965,
pp.1065–6
Building, 2 December 1966, pp.65–7
Architectural Review, December 1972, pp.362–70
A & U, December 1974, pp.73–128

1966–9
Private Houses
Dunstan Road, Oxford
Client: Lower Farm Housing Group
Architectural Review, January 1966, p.50
Architectural Review, September 1970, pp.186–8
Architecture d'Aujourd'hui, December/January
1971–2, pp.68–70

1966–71
Redcar Library**
Redcar, North Yorkshire
Client: Greater Teesdale Authority
Architectural Review, July 1971, pp.43–50
Baumeister, January 1974, pp.40–42
A & U, December 1974, pp.73–128

1966–73
Maidenhead Library
Maidenhead, Berkshire
Client: Maidenhead Borough Council
Listed: grade II
Architectural Review, May 1974, pp.256–67
Deutsche Bauzeitschrift, July 1976, pp.851–4
Glass Age, February 1977, pp.25–7
Technique des Travaux, July/August 1977,
pp.117–20
Industria delle costruzioni, July/August 1979,
pp.39–43
Geoffrey Tyack, Simon Bradley and Nikolaus
Pevsner, *The Buildings of England, Berkshire*, New
Haven & London, Yale University Press, 2010,
pp.371–2

1968
Thurmaston School
Thurmaston, Leicestershire
Client: Leicestershire County Council
Architects' Journal, 29 October 1969, pp.1081–92
Architecture d'Aujourd'hui, February/March
1971, pp.46–7

1968
Canberra Bell Tower***
Canberra, Australia
Client: UK Ministry of Works
Architects' Journal, 8 May 1968, pp.992–3
Architectural Design, June 1968, p.253

1968–72
St Andrew's College, Booterstown
Dublin, Republic of Ireland
Client: Board of Governors, St Andrew's College
Architectural Review, June 1976, pp.354–9
Baumeister, February 1977, pp.121–4
A & U, July 1979, pp.103–10

1968–77
Chalvedon housing
Basildon New Town, Essex
Client: Basildon Development Corporation
Architectural Review, September 1970, p.182
RIBA Journal, February 1976, p.50
Baumeister, July 1977, pp.628–31
Architects' Journal, 14 September 1977,
pp.485–502
Architects' Journal, 26 October 1977, p.785
Architecture d'Aujourd'hui, April 1978, pp.24–5
A & U, December 1978, pp.23–32
RIBA Journal, January 1979, pp.19–22

1968–2003
Arts Building and extension, Trinity College Dublin
Dublin, Republic of Ireland
Client: Trinity College Dublin
Building, 24 March 1978, p.36
Building Design, 23 June 1978, p.24
Architects' Journal, 15 November 1978, pp.914–16
RIBA Journal, January 1979, pp.23–6
Arup Journal, April 1979, pp.20–5
Architects' Journal, 18 July 1979, pp.121–35
A & U, October 1979, pp.83–95
Baumeister, December 1979, pp.1240–5

Keble

Industria delle costruzioni, December 1979,
pp.40–5
Architecture Today, October 2003, pp.20–5

1968
Basildon SW area study***
Client: Basildon Development Corporation
Architecture, June 1977, pp.18–19
Building, 3 June 1977, pp.68–71

1968–72
Nebenzahl House
Old City, Jerusalem, Israel
Client: Dr I. E. Nebenzahl
Architectural Review, August 1975, pp.108–15
Architecture d'Aujourd'hui, August 1975,
pp.108–15
Baumeister, December 1976, pp.1055–8
A & U, September 1977, pp.59–66
Architecture d'Aujourd'hui, April 1978,
pp.xiii–xiv
Industria delle costruzioni, November 1978, p.64–9

1969–1990
Oxford Centre for Management Studies/ Said Business School
Kennington, Oxford
Part listed Grade II
Client: University of Oxford/Templeton College
Architectural Review, August 1969, pp.136–9
Architects' Journal, 10 September 1969, pp.596–9
Architectural Forum, May 1970, pp.40–3
Architecture d'Aujourd'hui, December/January
1971–2, pp.72–4

1972–80
Residential accommodation, Keble College*
Keble College, Oxford
Client: Keble College, Oxford
Listed: Grade II*
Architectural Review, July 1973, pp.5–16 and
30–3

Arup Journal, June 1976, pp.31–5
Building Design, 6 May 1977, pp.18–19
Architectural Review, December 1977, pp.349–57
RIBA Journal, August 1978, p.320
Industria delle costruzioni, January 1979,
pp.66–70
Building Design, 31 October 1980, pp.27–8
Geoffrey Tyack, *Oxford: An Architectural Guide*,
Oxford, Oxford University Press, 1998, pp.324–5

1972–4
Habitat retail store and warehouse*
Wallingford, Berkshire
Client: Habitat Ltd
Financial Times, 30 July 1974, p.13
Architectural Review, August 1974, pp.74–9
Building, 16 August 1974, pp.62–6
Architectural Design, October 1974, pp.651–2
Baumeister, October 1976, pp.876–8
Financial Times, 11 November 1976, p.27
Architects' Journal, 2 April 1980, pp.647–8
RIBA Journal, June 1981, p.35

Habitat

1973
Plan Guinet***
Valescure, France
Client: Southern Real Estate

1973–90
Portsmouth Polytechnic library and development plan
Portsmouth, Hampshire
Client: Hampshire County Council

Architects' Journal, 26 July 1978, pp.156–7
Architectural Review, April 1979, pp.198–203
Architects' Journal, 4 April 1979, pp.683–99
A & U, October 1979, pp.96–106
Baumeister, December 1979, pp.1262–6
Architects' Journal, 24 January 1990, pp.44–51
and 55–7

1974–80
Felmore housing
Basildon New Town, Essex
Client: Basildon Development Corporation
Architects' Journal, 10 October 1979, pp.762–6
Building, 19 October 1979, pp.40–2
Building Design, 4 July 1980, pp.16–17
Building Design, 11 December 1981, p.16

1975–83
Cummins Engines Factory
Shotts, Lanarkshire
Client: Cummins Engine Co. Ltd
Listed: Grade A (Scottish listings)
Building, 10 November 1978, pp.94–8
RIBA Journal, January 1979, pp.15–18
Architectural Review, October 1979, pp.250–1
Architecture Intérieure – Créé, February/March
1981, pp.82–3
The Structural Engineer, October 1981,
pp.325–33
Architectural Review, February 1982, pp.31–9
Architects' Journal, 17 February 1982, pp.39–56
Building, 19 February 1982, pp.32–5
Observer Colour Supplement, 2 May 1982

Cummins

Architecture d'Aujourd'hui, June 1982, pp.40–5
Prospect (Scotland), Autumn 2006, pp.36–7

1975
Post Office headquarters***
St Martin's le-Grand, London
Client: Property Services Agency
Building, 21 March 1975, p.61
Architects' Journal, 26 March 1975, p.655
Architectural Review, July 1975, pp.4–7

1975
Whitmore Court
Basildon New Town, Essex
Client: Basildon Development Corporation
Building Design, 3 June 1977, pp.14–15
A & U, September 1977, pp.19–30

1977
British Airports Authority (BAA) Head Office***
Gatwick Airport, West Sussex
Client: BAA

1978
Johnson & Johnson Head Office***
Slough, Berkshire
Client: Johnson & Johnson

1979–2007
Collen House (2 phases)
Glencree, Co. Wicklow, Republic of Ireland
Client: Phase 1 – Mr and Mrs Lyall Collen; Phase 2 – Mrs Neil Collen
Architectural Review, January 1980, p.39
Architecture Today, November 2008, pp.14–17

1979–90
John Lewis, Kingston
Kingston upon Thames, London
Client: John Lewis Partnership
Building Design, 11 January 1980, p.22
RIBA Journal, February 1981, pp.48–9
Architects' Journal, 30 April 1986, p.18
Building, 14 September 1990, p.10
Arup Journal, Spring 1991, pp.10–13
Architects' Journal, 10 April 1991, pp.32–49

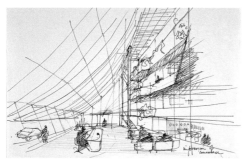

Johnson and Johnson

John Lewis

1980
Mary Rose Museum***
Portsmouth, Hampshire
Client: Mary Rose Trust
Architects' Journal, 3 December 1980, p.1074
Building, 5 December 1980, p.27
Museums Journal, June 1981, pp.11–17

1981
Abbey National Housing project***
Location
Client: Abbey National Building Society

1982–90
St Mary's Hospital
Town, Isle of Wight
Client: UK Department of Health and Social
Security/Wessex Regional Health Authority
Architects' Journal, 27 October 1982, pp.45–62
Architects' Journal, 7 May 1986, p.16
Architects' Journal, 3 August 1988, p.12
Architecture Today, June 1990, pp.46, 51–2
and 55
British Medical Journal, 22–29 December 1990,
pp.1423–5
Architects' Journal, 3 July 1991, pp.24–41
Industria delle costruzioni, November 1991,
pp.20–7
Building, 21 March 1997, pp.50–5

1982–5
National Gallery extension***
Trafalgar Square, London
Client: Trafalgar House Developments Ltd/
Property Services Agency
Financial Times, 24 August 1982, p.9
Architects' Journal, 25 August 1982, pp.62–7
Sunday Times, 29 August 1982
Architects' Journal, 15 September 1982, pp.60–3
Building, 22 October 1982, p.9
Architectural Review, December 1982, pp.19–25
The Times, 8 December 1983, p.2

Architectural Review, February 1984, pp.56–61
Observer, 1 April 1984, p.18
Architects' Journal, 27 May 1987, p.17
Charles Jencks, *The Prince, the Architects
and New Wave Monarchy*, London, Academy
Editions, 1988

1982–5
W. H. Smith headquarters
Swindon, Wiltshire
Client: W. H. Smith Ltd
Architects' Journal, 7 September 1983, p.43
Architectural Review, January 1984, p.30
RIBA Journal, March 1988, pp.5, 38–40
RIBA Journal, October 1996, pp.38–43

1982–4
Sainsbury's store
Canterbury, Kent
Client: J. Sainsbury Ltd
Architects' Journal, 13 October 1982, pp.44–6
Architectural Review, May 1983, pp.69–73
Architects' Journal, 20 June 1984, pp.25 and 27
Architects' Journal, 5 December 1984, pp.41–8

1983
**Thames Project (with Richard Rogers and
John Hawkes + Partners)*****
Client: Private initiative with Richard Rogers and
John Hawkes
Architectural Design, 56 (4) 1986, pp.10–15

1983–90
Hooke Park
Parnham, Dorset
Client: Parnham Trust
Building, 18 November 1983, p.9
Architects' Journal, 21/28 December 1983,
pp.22–59
Building, 4 October 1985, pp.30–1
Architects' Journal, 28 November 1985,
pp.115–29

Architectural Review, January 1986, p.50
Architects' Journal, 5 November 1986, p.17
Architectural Review, September 1990, pp.44–8
Building Research and Information, March/April
1998, pp.76–93

1983
British Telecom headquarters***

Milton Keynes, Buckinghamshire
Client: British Telecom

1985
Stoneyard Lane feasibility study***

Location
Client: London Docklands Development
Corporation

1985–6
National Garden Festival Pavilion**

Stoke-on-Trent, Staffordshire
Client: National Garden Festival 1986
Building Design, 30 November 1984, p.32

1986–2002
Burton House

Kentish Town, London
Client: Mr and Mrs R Burton
Architectural Review, September 1990, pp.39–43
Building Design, October 1991, pp.25–6
Catherine Slessor, *100 of the World's Best Houses*,
Mulgrave, Victoria, Australia, Images Publishing,
2011, pp.68–9 and 326

1986
Offices ***

Shaftesbury Avenue, London
Client: Standard Life Assurance Ltd
Architectural Review, January 1988, pp.63–4

1987
Offices***

Stag Place, London
Client: Land Securities plc
Architectural Review, January 1988, pp.57–8

1987
DLR stations and bridges

Docklands, London
Client: London Docklands Development
Corporation
Architecture Today, April 1990, pp.64–5
Architecture Today, July 1993, pp.16–18 and 21–2
Architects' Journal, 27 April 1994, pp.13–16

1988–90
Dover Heritage Centre

Dover, Kent
Client: Dover District Council
Architects' Journal, 23 November 1988, p.14
Building Design, 7 April 1989, p.12
Architecture Today, April 1991, pp.12–13
Building, 26 April 1991, pp.49–54

1988–90
North Pole Depot***

Location
Client: British Rail
Building Design, 8 December 1989, pp.1–2

1988–2000
British Embassy

Moscow, Russian Federation
Client: HM Foreign & Commonwealth Office
Architects' Journal, 20 October 1994, pp.8–9
Building, 25 June 1999, pp.46–51
Royal Academy Magazine, Spring 2000, pp.52–5
RIBA Journal, May 2000, pp.38–48
Architects' Journal, 18 May 2000, pp.6–7
Architecture Today, October 2000, pp.82–6
Jeremy Melvin, *The New British Embassy,
Moscow*, London, Foreign & Commonwealth
Office, 2000.

1989
Compton Verney Opera House***
Compton Verney, Northamptonshire
Client: Compton Verney Opera Project
Architectural Design, vol. 60, 1990, pp.ii–vi

1990
Grenoble University Master Plan
Grenoble, France
Client: University of Grenoble
Building Design, 6 April 1990

Grenoble University

1991–9
Whitworth Art Gallery extension
Manchester
Client: University of Manchester
Building Design, 9 July 1993, p.8

1991–8
Dublin Dental Hospital
Dublin, Republic of Ireland
Client: Dublin Dental Hospital
Irish Architect, November/December 1998,
pp.23–7
Architecture Today, February 1999, pp.30–6
Hospital Development, April 1999, pp.14–29

1992–5
Techniquest, Cardiff Bay
Cardiff
Client: Techniquest
Building, 21 July 1995, pp.34–9

1993
East London Line extension stations***
East London
Client: London Underground Ltd
RIBA Journal, July 1993, pp.22–7

1995–7
Selly Oak Colleges Library
Birmingham
Client: Selly Oak Colleges

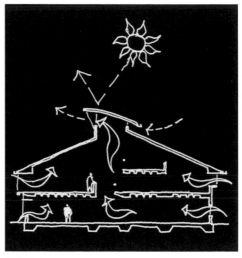

Selly Oak

1996 and 2011
Health Centre
London, Hoxton
Client: Lawson Practice

1996–2001
Institute of Technology Tralee
Tralee, Co. Kerry, Republic of Ireland
Client: Institute of Technology Tralee/
Department of Education (Ireland)